Anthony J. Marinelli

CONSCIENCE AND CATHOLIC FAITH

Love and Fidelity

PAULIST PRESS
New York and Mahwah, N.J.

Library of Congress Cataloging-in-Publication Data

Marinelli, Anthony J.
    Conscience and Catholic faith: love and fidelity / Anthony J.
Marinelli.
        p.   cm.
    Includes biographical references.
    ISBN 0-8091-3263-X
    1. Conscience—Religious aspects—Catholic Church. 2. Catholic
Church—Doctrines. I. Title.
BJ1278.C66M37 1991
241'. 1—dc20   91-27081
                                                                     CIP

Published by Paulist Press
997 Macarthur Boulevard
Mahwah, NJ 07430

Printed and bound in the
United States of America

Contents

Dedicated to
Julia Marinelli,
George Deas and
Pat McDonough

with gratitude and love

Introduction

Recently I was leading a workshop on the meaning of conscience in the Catholic tradition. When I had finished describing the contributions of Vatican II to the understanding of conscience, a woman raised her hand and asked, "Does this mean that we can do what we choose and not what the church teaches?" I asked the other participants if they would like to try to answer that question (since I thought that I had already explained it as well as I could). The responses were wide in range. A woman in her fifties said, "Of course we have to obey the teaching of the church. The pope is Christ's representative, not me or you. How can we know that what we do is really right if we don't believe in the teaching of the church." A middle-aged gentleman suggested that ever since Vatican II the teaching of the church was to be understood like the advice of a parent to an adult child: it was to be respected and listened to, but the decision was always one's own. A young woman offered that what mattered to her was her relationship with Jesus and God, not with the pope. "He seems like a good and holy man, but he's only human. It's tough to take advice on marriage from someone who has never been married."

Such is the state of affairs in the church today. The relationship between conscience and the teaching of the pope and bishops is one that has left many Catholics confused. For some, the responsibility to obey the teaching of the church has been replaced by the call to follow their conscience. The expression "Follow your conscience" seems to mean many

1

different things to different people. This book is a very modest attempt to shed some light on the confusion.

The first two chapters of the book focus on the very meaning of conscience. Chapter 1 gives a theological perspective. Chapter 2 presents a psychological overview. Chapter 3 treats special themes related to conscience: freedom, grace, virtue and sin. The last two chapters examine the two main sources for a Catholic Christian conscience: the teaching of Jesus and the role of the church.

In writing this book, I hope to synthesize four areas of essential concern: first, the teaching of the church, primarily as it is reflected in the documents of the Second Vatican Council; second, contemporary theological insights into the nature and role of conscience; third, the input of psychology and developmental theory; fourth, the moral "vision" of the gospel. It is my hope that this book will make the insights of these various sources accessible to the non-specialized reader and provide a broad basis for understanding conscience in relation to Catholic faith.

1

Conscience: A Catholic Theological Perspective

"I know you believe you understand what you think I said. But I am not sure you realize that what you heard is not what I meant."

I don't know the author of the statement above, but he or she may well have been thinking of conscience when saying it. The task of understanding and following one's conscience in the church today seems to be characterized by confusion and competing claims. Therefore we shall try to begin at the beginning and seek a basis for discussion. What is conscience? Webster's Dictionary says that it is "knowledge or feeling of right and wrong; the faculty, power or principle which decides on the lawfulness or unlawfulness of his actions, with a compulsion to do right; moral judgment that prohibits or opposes the violation of a previously recognized moral principle."

That's quite a mouthful. According to this definition, conscience is knowledge or feeling, it is a faculty or power, and it is a judgment. These are three distinct things in one definition. And this is only the first definition listed. This is no small problem, because often when we speak of conscience, we are speaking of different but highly related realities. In one of the finest works on the issue, *Principles for a Catholic Morality,* Fr. Timothy O'Connell distinguishes among three different dimensions of conscience. For the sake of simplicity he refers to them as conscience/1, conscience/2, and conscience/ 3.[1]

3

Conscience/1 could be described as the fundamental human drive to seek and do the good. Human beings are unique kinds of beings. They are capable of love, understanding and choice. We may be able to train our dog to be obedient, but, as far as we know, they and the rest of the animal kingdom have no self-knowledge and awareness. They do not choose what and who they will become. They cannot betray or fulfill themselves. Human beings can. A person who shows no such desire to seek and do the good, to become a good person, is generally perceived to be morally, socially or emotionally ill. Conscience/1 then is conscience as a unique faculty or characteristic of human persons. It is the very direction and orientation of the human person to seek and do the good. In religious terms, this orientation to the good is also the impulse of the heart toward God. St. Augustine gave his classic description of this orientation: "You have made us for yourself, O Lord, and our hearts are restless until they rest in you." Augustine's insight describes the fundamental insight of Christianity concerning the meaning of humanity. We are created by and for God.

Contemporary theologians call this dimension of being "transcendence." Humans are capable of going beyond themselves in love and knowledge. Through these capacities, people become "more" human and reach beyond themselves in order to find themselves. The human openness to knowledge and love is an unlimited orientation in life. One never knows fully or loves completely. *But all acts of knowing and loving move us ultimately in the direction of the goal of our being: God.* We realize the true meaning and destiny of our being insofar as we cooperate with its fundamental orientation. In other words, humans possess a capacity to choose or to deny the basic direction of their life. This fundamental freedom which allows us to say yes or no to the basic orientation toward God and the good is intrinsic to our being human. Or, as the fathers of the church described it at the Second Vatican Council:

4

In the depths of his conscience, man detects a law which he does not impose upon himself, but which holds him to obedience. Always summoning him to love good and avoid evil, the voice of conscience can when necessary speak to his heart more specifically: do this, shun that. For man has in his heart a law written by God. To obey it is the very dignity of man; according to it, he will be judged (*Gaudium et Spes*, n. 16).

If human beings have an innate drive to seek and do the good, they must learn to distinguish the good from the bad or the truly good from the apparent good. They must develop a sensitivity to human values. They gain this from the world, culture, family, church, society and ideas that they are exposed to. It is on this level that we can speak of an "informed conscience" or, as O'Connell refers to it, conscience/2. On this level, individual consciences will vary, sometimes dramatically, because of their sensitivity to some values and insensitivity to others. In our own country, we see this plainly when mature, responsible men and women of good will differ on their assessment of the morality of abortion, the arms race, capital punishment, sex outside of marriage, and a whole host of social and moral issues. Conscience/1 is, in a sense, a "gift," that which is universally endowed. I didn't ask to have it. It's simply there. Conscience/2, on the other hand, is very different. It is an achievement, an accomplishment. *It requires training, education, formation.* It is on this level that we can distinguish different "types" of conscience, one of which is a Catholic Christian conscience. If conscience must be formed, then it will vary somewhat depending on the factors that shape it. One's sensitivity to values will be different depending on the moral and spiritual climate in which one is raised. It is here where the teaching of the church and the wisdom of the Christian community come to play their vital roles. They possess, at their best, an exceptional ability to distill and com-

5

municate values. On this level, we refer not only to the teaching of the magisterium, the pope and the bishops, but also to the local communities of faith, the parish and especially the community of the family as the primary educator of values. But the church is by no means the sole teacher of values. Human values exist wherever human beings live in fidelity to their own humanity. *The church can learn from the world and from those outside the faith.* There exists a very important "reciprocity of consciences." It is essential that we learn from one another.

> In fidelity to conscience, Christians are joined with the rest of men in the search for truth and for the genuine solution to the numerous problems that arise in the life of individuals and from social relationships (*Gaudium et Spes*, n. 16).

Conscience/2 is truly the art of being fully human. It is the human person sensitized and aware of human values and capable of responding to those values. But saints and seers are rare, and part of the problem lies within the factors that form our sense of right and wrong. We learn from our parents, culture and church not only their values, but their disvalues as well. If I grow up in a bigoted family and a bigoted culture, it will be very difficult for me to see beyond those bigotries. Where will I learn to be accepting? Thus the informed conscience will never be fully informed. In a world that is radically imperfect, in a pilgrim church, and in limited human beings, the formation of conscience is always an ongoing reality. There are always "moral blindspots" in the society in which we live. (This is, of course, also true for the church. This does not mean that a church doctrine is necessarily in error, but, more likely, church practices may reflect the moral blindspots of their time and age—for example, the acceptance of slavery, sexism, intolerance of other religious beliefs, etc.)

Nor is the formation of conscience simply a matter of

obtaining the right information (although that is certainly an important step). For example, I may know the church's teaching on the morality of abortion and be familiar with the arguments and be willing to obey it. But until I truly appreciate the values behind the church's teaching, I have only a notional or *conceptual knowledge* of right and wrong. A more mature conscience recognizes "why" something is right or wrong. It is sensitive and aware of the values at stake. The person accepts these values as their own. This is an *evaluative knowledge* born of human experience and insight.

For a Christian, the teaching of Jesus and the church and the values and wisdom of the Christian community will always have a role of unique importance in the formation of conscience. We will examine these in greater depth later in this book. For now, suffice it to say that Christians believe that Jesus is truly the "light of the world," "the way, the truth and the life," the fullness of humanity. In his words, deeds, death and resurrection, we believe that we can find the richest path to the development of our minds, hearts and spirit. Nor is our faith in Christ a faith in something in the past. Christians believe that Jesus' death and resurrection allowed him to be present in a new and powerful way through the Spirit. This Spirit lives in all men and women but in a unique way through the church, the body of Christ in the world. Therefore, we can look to this community for guidance in the Spirit and even for direct teaching about moral issues. The entire church, all baptized Christians, share in the vocation of the church as a teacher of values. This is especially true for parents who have the greatest impact on the future of their children. The leaders of the church, the pope and bishops, have a unique role to teach on behalf of the entire community in matters of faith and morals. They have a unique authority in the formation of Christian conscience.

If conscience/1 is the human drive toward the good, and conscience/2 is seeking the truth that forms and informs, then conscience/3 is the conscience in judgment and action. *Conscience/3* decides about the course of action to be taken

7

in a specific situation. Conscience/3 realizes that its judgments and decisions are not necessarily objectively correct. It is served by conscience/2 which is not God. But it must do what it believes to be the right and true thing. It not only *can* do it, it *must* do it. This is the sacred nature of conscience. It is for this reason that the Second Vatican Council says:

> Conscience is the most secret core and sanctuary of a man. There he is alone with God whose voice echoes in his depths (*Gaudium et Spes*, n. 16).

It is in this sense that a person must follow his or her conscience, with the assumption that conscience is genuinely seeking to find and do the truth. Conscience at times may force a person to act against commonly held standards of right and wrong. Following one's conscience under such circumstances is not *easy* or convenient. But it must be done. (We will say much more about "following one's conscience" later.)

Other Aspects of Conscience

The Erroneous Conscience. The fact that a person has genuinely sought to discover the good does not mean that in fact he or she will necessarily find it. A person may be convinced that his or her actions are true and good when objectively, in fact, they are not. In a world of moral ambiguity, this will not be uncommon. What then? Should a person follow his or her conscience? One can do nothing else. For an erroneous conscience does not know it is erroneous. It sincerely believes that it is doing what is best. The tradition of the Catholic Church strongly supports the rights and dignity of the "erroneous conscience." This was reiterated at the Second Vatican Council in the *Pastoral Constitution on the Church in the Modern World*:

8

Conscience frequently errs from invincible ignorance without losing its dignity (*Gaudium et Spes*, n. 16).

"Invincible" ignorance is ignorance that one cannot be held responsible for. Thus the erroneous conscience retains its dignity only if its error is not one that could be easily overcome.

The Lax Conscience. The erroneous conscience is not to be confused with the lax conscience, which exerts no effort in coming to know the truth or allows laziness and indifference to deaden its capacity to know the good. The lax conscience is one that has slowly and gradually allowed itself to be seduced by selfishness. It makes no strong claims of right or wrong. It simply falls into a habit of moral dullness. Its sin is often one of complacency. Thus, while Vatican II upheld the dignity of the erroneous conscience, it went on to say: "The same cannot be said of a man who cares but little for truth and goodness, or of a conscience which by degrees grows practically sightless as a result of habitual sin" (*Gaudium et Spes*, n. 16).

The Scrupulous Conscience. For some people, conscience is a terror that haunts, a burden almost too heavy to bear. These are persons with a scrupulous conscience. For such persons there is little true freedom. Every mistake, even the smallest, carries with it a disproportionate amount of guilt. For the scrupulous person, conscience is not so much sensitivity to value as it is feelings of guilt. We will look at this conscience further when we examine some of the psychological perspectives on conscience.

Conscience and the Natural Law

We have emphasized the notion that conscience is "built into" the nature of being human. This dynamism of our being which seeks the good is closely related to the notion of the "natural law." Natural law is an important part of our understanding of conscience because it claims that goodness is not something that is revealed to a unique group, nor is it something that is determined by each individual. It is rather something that has universal appeal to our humanity. It is "revealed" to all humans open to it. As such, it is not a "law" as much as it is a principle of our humanity. It is this principle that Paul refers to when he writes:

> When Gentiles who do not have the law keep it as by instinct, these men although without the law serve as a law for themselves. They show that the demands of the law are written in their hearts. Their conscience bears witness together with that law, and their thoughts will accuse or defend them on the day when . . . God will pass judgment on the secrets of men through Christ Jesus (Rom 2:14–16).

The law that is "written in their hearts" is not unlike the God "whose voice echoes in his depths" (Vatican II) or the law detected by man "which he does not impose on himself" (Vatican II). It is based on the belief that all men and women are created with a fundamental orientation to seek and do the good. Or again, in the words of Vatican II:

> In a wonderful manner conscience reveals that law which is fulfilled by love of God and neighbor (*Gaudium et Spes*, n. 16).

For Christians, belief in the natural law is a recognition that human values do not originate arbitrarily in each individual. Right and wrong are not simply a matter of opinion or cultural conditioning. Rather, right and wrong are rooted in transcendent values such as love, justice, human dignity, integrity and compassion. The values, nurtured in the human heart, are the "call of God." Yet, although Christians understand this law as rooted in the divine plan, it precedes faith and does not presuppose it. The natural law is precisely that which leads the non-believer to know and do the good. Thus, in Paul's explanation, all can stand before the judgment of God because of the existence of the natural law written in their heart. Thus in Matthew 25, when Jesus describes the last judgment, he explains that the non-believers (called "the nations") may also be saved. The criteria: how have they treated the least of the brethren. In other words, there is a "natural law" of love and justice to which they will be held accountable.

The natural law is not something extrinsic and imposed from without. It is part of the created order, yet Christians believe that it reveals the divine plan of the creator. In defending the human right to religious liberty, Vatican II explained:

> . . . the highest law of human life is the divine law—eternal, objective and universal—whereby God orders, directs and governs the entire universe and all the ways of the human community by a plan conceived in wisdom and love. Man has been made by God to participate in this law, with the result that, under the gentle disposition of divine providence, he can come to perceive ever increasingly the unchanging truth (*Declaration on Religious Freedom*, n. 3).

The meaning of natural law for the church is rooted in the theology of Thomas Aquinas who distinguished three levels at which the natural law applied, depending on the "end" or goal. At the first level was the law that united humans with all creation (self-conservation); second, that which we share with the animal kingdom (reproduction and care of offspring); third, that which is unique to human nature (knowledge of truth and relationships). Today many theologians emphasize this final tendency as the heart of the natural law. This aspect of the natural law places priority on the dignity of the person as a thinking and loving agent. It places the biological "laws

11

of nature" in the context of the entire person and the laws of love and responsibility. As such, O'Connell believes that the natural law will have the following characteristics:

1. *It is a realism.* Right and wrong is based on that which *really* fulfills our nature and enhances the good of the entire human community. An action is not good because a law says it is. This is the mistake of legalism. It has inherent value to it. The fulfillment of the law is love, not obedience. Nor is an action good simply because *I believe* it is good. This is the error of subjectivism. Its value lies in itself, not in my perception of it. There is an objectivity to human values.

2. *It is experiential.* Goodness is evaluated by the court of human experience and wisdom. This is not to say that divine revelation plays no part in helping us understand what is truly good. But the fact remains that it is human beings who must decide. Our experience of what is truly good enables us, as a community, to evaluate and judge the good. The discovery of the truly good is something that is performed by human beings trying to uncover the true direction and goal of the natural law.

3. *It is consequential.* In order to determine the morality of an action, one must look at its consequences. How does this action affect myself and the rest of the community? The consequences will at times be very difficult to ascertain, but they will determine the goodness of an action. For Christians, the criteria must include whether the consequences will enhance the dignity and worth of those affected. It is important to note here that the consequences are not necessarily those immediately discernible. Rather, it is the long-range consequences that we are interested in.

4. *It is historical.* Our understanding of the good is situated in time and history. Human nature is not simply an abstraction that is universally true. Humans are situated in certain times and cultures which affect our understanding of the good. Thus it is important to recognize that our understanding of the good will always be somewhat determined by when and where we exist in the world. Therefore, the natural law is

not necessarily immutable. Thus, while certain principles may remain universally valid (do good; avoid evil), our understanding of the good is situated in time and can, in theory, change. (Such an approach represents a major departure in method within the Catholic Church. Until recently, the church's approach was "classicist"—that is, it believed that it was possible to know and understand the truth from a universal, absolute point. Some theologians continue to hold this position.)

5. Finally, *it is proportional*. The natural law must choose between competing goods or evils. It must seek out what is best or what is least evil in a given circumstance. The right action is the one that seeks out that which is proportionally best. O'Connell relates this to the virtue of prudence. Because we are limited, finite persons who cannot achieve all the good we may seek, we must learn to make judgments that maximize our capacity to love.[2]

Obstacles

Discovering the good is not as simple as listening to the voice of the natural law inside us. The Canadian theologian Bernard Lonergan describes the process as fourfold: experience, understanding, judgment and decision. By experience, Lonergan means living with eyes open to life in all its dimensions. It encompasses all aspects of life: intellectual, emotional, spiritual, physical, psychological. Understanding seeks to give meaning to one's experience. It interprets the experience. Judgment places that understanding before the scrutiny of others. How does my perception fit in with the perception of others? In light of the dialogue with others, what should my judgment be? Finally, there is decision. In light of my experience, understanding and judgment, I must act. Thus, for Lonergan, the precepts for living a truly human existence are: Be attentive. Be intelligent. Be reasonable. Be loving.

There are obstacles to such living. Lonergan calls them

biases, and he discerns four.[3] First, there is the "dramatic bias." This is the psychological disorders and immaturity created by a fear of self-knowledge. Fear of self-knowledge creates personal blindspots that inhibit and block genuine human and moral development. This is not to be confused with psychological problems that are chemically or environmentally based. According to psychologist Abraham Maslow, "Freud's greatest discovery is that the great cause of psychological illness is the fear of the knowledge of oneself."[4]

The second bias is called the bias of egoism. This is the temptation to judge the good solely as that which is good for *me*. It thus escapes the paradox of love which seeks the good of others as well as of oneself. Thus, if the county is planning on building a home for retarded adults next to my home, I oppose it because I fear it will not be good for my property values. It is not good because it is not good for me. The bias of egoism is a one-sided, self-centered view of the good.

The third bias is the group bias. From this perspective the good is determined by how it impacts my group. Thus, white South Africans may seek to keep apartheid intact for the good of their group, or the National Rifle Association opposes a ban on assault weapons to protect the group's position. The foreign policy of the United States is sometimes based solely on its interests in other countries.

The fourth bias is the bias of common sense. Common sense is a particularly important way of knowing and understanding the truth, but it can also become an obstacle to the truth. Common sense stops at the level of experience and interpretation. It fails to critically judge its own insights. Common sense tells us that the sun revolves around the earth. Its concerns are practical and immediate. However, such thinking cannot plan for the future or learn from the past unless it is willing to do "abstract" thinking. For Lonergan, knowing and doing the truth demands going beyond the realm of common sense to critical thinking and judgments.

Lonergan's analysis of human knowing and the obstacles to such insight reveal the heart of the meaning of conscience:

human beings are oriented toward the good and the true, but we are in danger of missing it. Because of this danger, conscience must be informed and formed. We will leave it to later chapters to examine the factors that shape Christian conscience.

Summary

1. Conscience is the human capacity to know and do the good.
2. Conscience can be divided into three realms of meaning.
3. Conscience/1 is the innate human drive to seek the good and the true. It is an in-built dynamism of human nature.
4. Conscience/2 is conscience as it is actually formed and sensitized to values.
5. Conscience/3 is the actual judgment and decision of the individual. It is conscience in action.
6. All people have a conscience. Christian conscience is characterized by its faith in Jesus Christ and the life in the Spirit.
7. Catholic Christian conscience must be rooted in the teaching of Jesus and the wisdom of the Christian community, especially attentive to the teaching of the magisterium.
8. An erroneous conscience is one that sincerely seeks the truth but has arrived at an objectively false judgment. Such a conscience, although in error, retains its essential dignity.
9. A lax conscience is one that has grown apathetic, dull and insensitive to value.
10. A scrupulous conscience is an unhealthy conscience with a disproportionate experience of guilt and shame.
11. The "natural law" recognizes that human nature is drawn to the good by a law "written in the heart." All persons are capable, to some degree, of knowing the good. It emphasizes that values are not arbitrary or subjective.

12. An understanding of natural law today will recognize that it is a realism, it is experiential, it is consequential, it is historical, and it is proportional.
13. We are in danger of missing the call to goodness. Bernard Lonergan describes four biases that blind us to the good: the dramatic bias, the bias of egoism, the group bias, and the bias of common sense.

Questions for Review

1. Describe the three different levels of conscience and how they function.
2. Define "transcendence."
3. What is meant by the statement in *Gaudium et Spes* that "man detects a law which he does not impose upon himself, but which holds him to obedience?"
4. How would Christian conscience be distinct from non-Christian conscience? How would it be similar?
5. What is meant by a reciprocity of consciences?
6. What is meant by an erroneous conscience? What is the difference between vincible and invincible ignorance?
7. What is meant by "conceptual" and "evaluative" knowledge?
8. What is a lax conscience?
9. What is meant by "natural law"?
10. Explain O'Connell's five characteristics of natural law.
11. Name and briefly explain Lonergan's four precepts for living a fully human life.
12. What are Lonergan's four "biases"? Explain.

For Personal Reflection and Discussion

1. Analyze your own value system. Consider those things that are really important to you, that you publicly profess and try to live.

Rank the following in order of importance:

good marriage (present or future)   faith
friends   integrity
wealth   health
good looks   family
popularity   athletic ability
good job   comfortable life

In what ways do you affirm these values in your life? Who and what have been the most important influences on your values? How have they influenced you?

2. Give examples of how you perceive Lonergan's biases at work in your life and experience of the world.

Suggested Reading

Häring, Bernard. *Free and Faithful in Christ, Vol 1.* New York: Crossroad, 1982 (particularly Chapter 6).

O'Connell, Timothy. *Principles for a Catholic Morality.* New York: Seabury Press, 1976 (Chapter 8).

2

Conscience: Psychological and Developmental Perspectives

Having looked briefly at a theological description of conscience, we must now turn our attention to the psychological make-up of conscience. It is important to note at the beginning that there should be no inherent conflict between theological and psychological perspectives. Both of them strive to understand the same phenomenon: the human capacity to know and do the good. Where there is conflict, there must be dialogue in order to better ascertain the truth that each seeks to articulate.

The Id, the Ego and the Superego

"Thus conscience does make cowards of us all and the native hue of resolution is sicklied o'er with the pale cast of thought."

With those words Hamlet decides not to kill himself. His conscience has made him a coward. However, Hamlet has not responded to the call of conscience. He has responded to the fear of the superego. Perhaps the most consistent misunderstanding of conscience is to identify it with the psychological mechanism that Freud called the superego. Freud divided the human personality into three parts: the id, the superego and the ego. The *id* is the instinctual drive for pleasure. It works on the basic principle: seek pleasure, avoid pain. It is a bundle of instincts and drives that are his or her id. The drive and need to be fed, held, caressed, be warm, clean, have its diaper changed are all functions of the id. Of itself, the id is savagely self-centered. In a baby or a small child, such self-centered behavior is perfectly normal, and one would not think of criticizing a small child for being "selfish." This instinctual drive for pleasure, which includes one's sexuality, must of course find limits if the child is to develop into a mature person, capable of loving others. These are the functions of the superego and the ego.

The *superego* is the internalized commands of authority telling the child what he or she can or cannot do, what is right and what is wrong. The superego works from the position of authority. It does not develop in the child a true sense of *why* something is right or wrong. Within the child is a powerful need to be loved and accepted. If he or she violates the voice of the superego, there is a corresponding sense of love withdrawal and guilt. The superego is usually dominated by the authority of the parent, but it includes as well the voice of the teacher, the church, and other authority as well. The superego is an important aspect of personality that helps place limits on a child and give it a sense of discipline as well as keep him or her safe. For example, a small child doesn't really know the dangers of walking out into the street without a parent, but it does know (or should) the power of the command to never go in the street without mother or father. The superego is performing an extremely useful function. A child with little or no superego qualities places no limits on his or her drive for pleasure and will always be a disciplinary problem. On the other hand, a child who is only given orders and never told why will tend to develop a rigid, non-spontaneous personality incapable of responding creatively to new situations.

As a child grows older, he or she becomes more capable of recognizing *why* something is right or wrong beyond the commands and rules of the superego. (The church has traditionally said that this process begins around age seven: the age of reason. Studies from the field of psychology indicate that this is a fairly accurate assessment if we see it as a beginning and not some type of magical new-found capacity.) In time a person, very slowly and gradually, begins to recognize and appreciate the *values* behind the rules. He or she begins to think and decide for himself or herself more and more. This is the function of the *ego*. The ego is not a pejorative term, as it often is used popularly. It does not denote self-centeredness. It is, instead, the "self," the "I" in the best sense of those words. It is the referee between the id and the superego. It is the capacity of our selves to integrate all the various dimensions of our being. Needless to say, this is never done fully and completely. It is the ego that is aware of the impulses of the id and the prohibitions of the superego and makes decisions about what is truly good and best. As a person matures, his or her ego becomes more dominant, more in charge of his or her life. In this sense, persons become more themselves.

Conscience and the Id, Superego and Ego

What is the relationship between conscience and the id, superego and ego? There are some, including Freud himself, who identify the superego with conscience. According to this perspective, conscience is primarily the values of the community as they are communicated through the parent and other authority figures and internalized by the child. It is important to note that *this is not what the church means by a mature conscience*. If superego is related to conscience, it is at best the immature conscience, the conscience as a bud, but one that has in no way flowered. From a psychological perspective, Christian conscience is much more related to the ego. It is the mature self that decides, not the immature self guided by fear of love-withdrawal or by guilt. The difference between the two is truly the difference between day and night. In an article entitled "Conscience and Superego: A Key Distinction," John W. Glaser distinguishes the following differences between superego and true, mature conscience:[1]

Superego	Conscience
commands that an act be performed for approval, in order to make oneself lovable, accepted; fear of love withdrawal is the basis	invites to action, to love, and in this very act of other-directed commitment to co-create self-value
introverted: the thematic center is a sense of one's own value	extroverted: the thematic center is the value which invites . . .
static: does not grow, cannot learn; cannot function creatively in a new situation; merely repeats a basic command	dynamic: an awareness and sensitivity to value which develops and grows; a mind-set which can precisely function in a new situation
authority-figure-oriented: not a question of perceiving, and responding to a value, but of obeying authority's command blindly	value-oriented: the value or disvalue is perceived and responded to, regardless of whether authority has commanded or not
"atomized" units of activity are its object	individual acts are seen in their importance as part of a larger process or pattern
past-oriented: primarily concerned with cleaning up the record with regard to past acts	future-oriented: creative, sees the past as having a future and helping to structure this future as a better future

Superego	Conscience
urge to be punished and thereby earn reconciliation	sees the need to repair by structuring the future orientation toward the value in question (which includes making good past harms)
rapid transition from severe isolation, guilt feelings, etc., to a sense of self-value accomplished by confessing to an authority figure	a sense of the gradual process of growth that characterizes all dimensions of genuine personal development
possible great disproportion between guilt experienced and the value in question: extent of guilt depends more on the weight of authority figure and "volume" with which he speaks rather than the density of the value in question	experience of guilt proportionate to the importance of the value in question, even though authority may have never addressed this specific issue

The implications of these distinctions are profound for moral and spiritual development. In order to help train conscience and not only superego, one must do more than communicate rules and commands. One must sensitize to values. A person who has been raised to believe that conscience is the same as superego (and it does not seem uncommon) will be unduly attached to guilt, commands, laws, cultural standards, and will lack the creativity to truly respond in love. To recall the words of Vatican II, conscience is the place where a person is "alone with God, whose voice echoes in his depths." But when is the voice the voice of God and when is it the voice of one's parents or teachers or culture or of a distorted God. The **superego has a voice of** its own, and because of its great power it may seem to be the voice of God indeed. It commands, punishes, and reconciles with great emotional power. But it acts more as a prison than as a liberator or savior. This is not to say that the superego is unimportant, but it is not the mature conscience. And as Paul wrote to the early church in Corinth, "When I was a child I used to talk like a child, think like a child, reason like a child. When I became a man I put childish ways aside" (1 Cor 13:11). In order for the conscience to develop, the power of the superego must diminish and the power of the ego must increase. This does not mean that laws, commands, teaching of parents and church become irrelevant. To the contrary, they become more relevant than ever because the mature conscience is able to discern what it is that makes them truly valuable. It is able to recognize the insight and value that inspired these voices of authority.

Guilt and Conscience

The superego thrives on guilt and authority. As such, it can be a very effective way of controlling people's lives. Religions or individual preachers who seek to put the fear of God into people are often much more interested in control than they are in faith, hope or love. Scrupulosity is often a result of such a religious upbringing. This was not an uncommon part of religious development within the Catholic Church before the Second Vatican Council. For many Catholics, confession before Mass was a necessary prerequisite for receiving communion. Often the emphasis was placed on one's sinful unworthiness, and this affected not only self-images but images of God as well. In confession one was obliged to confess not only one's sins but to number the offenses. Such meticulousness tends to breed guilt and scrupulosity. As Glaser suggests, it leads to a disproportionate amount of guilt determined not by the real value offended but by the depth of the "voice of God." Such guilt, psychologically speaking, is neurotic. It does not correspond to the reality at hand.

23

Is there such a thing as healthy guilt in a healthy conscience? A healthy, mature conscience must also experience guilt if it is truly sensitive to values. It is this very sensitivity that cries out when one has offended one's own values or hurt another. Conscience cannot sit idly by. A mature conscience is incapable of ignoring the harm that it has done. The difference is in its response. The guilt is proportionate to the harm done and seeks to repair and grow from the situation.

Jean Piaget

If the goal of moral formation is the development of a healthy, mature conscience rooted in strong ego strengths and increasingly free from the unconscious controls of the immature superego and id, we must ask how this process takes place. The work of two men have dominated this field—Jean Piaget and Lawrence Kohlberg. Both men studied the process of moral reasoning in their subjects and concluded that moral growth is not simply taught. It is a developmental task, with clear boundaries of growth. Neither Piaget nor Kolberg was interested in observing behavior. Both wanted to know *why* people did what they did or thought as they thought. Two people who behave in exactly the same fashion may be light years apart in moral maturity depending on why they do as they do.

Piaget interviewed children between the ages of six and twelve, and was able to identify two distinct stages in the child's moral judgments. The first he called "heteronomous" and the second "autonomous." Children in these two different stages have very different notions of right and wrong. The heteronomous stage derives its rules, laws, and prohibitions completely from outside itself. Piaget called this type of morality "moral realism." It views something as right or wrong based solely on the fact that the rule comes from an authority figure. There is no sense of the value behind the rule, only the rule itself which admits of no exceptions. Right and wrong are often determined by their "material consequence" more than the underlying motives. Thus five year old Sean may believe that it is worse to drop a plate and break it while clearing the table for mom than it is to break a smaller plate while sneaking a cookie that mom has forbidden. In the heteronomous stage, there is little sense of the motive of one's behavior; only the consequences matter. (There are obvious connections here to the superego.)

In the autonomous stage (often achieved around the age of seven or eight), a child begins to develop an awareness of motives as the underlying principle of moral behavior. He or she perceives rules no longer simply as the imposition of authority but within the context of the group who share the rules. In other words, through social interaction the child begins to recognize the importance of rules for social interaction and fairness. He or she begins to see the *why* behind the rules.

Lawrence Kohlberg

Lawrence Kohlberg developed his theory of moral reasoning over a period of twenty years. Over these years he conducted interviews with one hundred boys and followed his subjects' development. Kohlberg concluded that moral reasoning developed through three levels which he subdivided into six stages. The following represents a summary of the six stages.

Level One: Pre-Conventional

STAGE ONE: FEAR OF PUNISHMENT

The first and most fundamental stage is fear of punishment. At this stage, a person decides based on whether or not he or she will be caught and punished for actions. Authority determines morality. Obviously, small children will often act on this level, but adults are by no means immune from it. Driving down the highway at 70 mph and slowing to 55 mph when I see a policeman in the rear-view mirror is an example of adult stage one behavior. Threatening children with early bedtime is an example of stage one motivation in parenting. Threatening the faithful with the pains of hell for missing mass on Sunday is an example of stage one motivation for religious leaders.

STAGE TWO: DESIRE FOR REWARD

The second stage is the reverse side of the coin. If the stage one person asks "Will I get caught?" the stage two person wants to know: "What's in it for me?" In stage two, the person decides based on self-interest. This person is willing to do for others as long as they are willing to do for him or her. Thus, a parent may offer rewards or positive reinforcement for a child's good behavior. "If you eat your dinner, you can have dessert" appeals to stage two reasoning. Church leaders appeal to this level when they offer the rewards of heaven to those who follow the laws of the church or the commandments.

Level Two: Conventional Morality

STAGE THREE: DESIRE TO BE LIKED BY OTHERS

At stage three a person's thinking is dominated by pleasing others. This stage could be called the "good boy/nice girl stage." This person is concerned with being accepted by others in the group or by authority. Thus a student who wants to be liked by the teacher is thinking on stage three level. This stage often calls for conformity, in order to fit in. Parents who reinforce good behavior with emotional acceptance appeal to children on this stage. Religious leaders who speak in terms of "good Catholics" are often appealing to this stage. Teenagers, often known for their rebellion, are in fact often on this stage. They have simply shifted their allegiance from traditional authorities to their peers. They want to be liked by their friends, and thus they achieve a "non-conforming conformity."

STAGE FOUR: RESPECT FOR LAW AND ORDER

The stage four person appreciates the importance of rules and order in order for society to function. Unlike, the stage one person, he or she does not obey rules out of fear of punishment. Rather, there is a genuine respect for the rules themselves. The stage four person is devoted to the system. Loyalty is his or her chief virtue. On this level, one fulfills one's duty and obligations. Parents who emphasize the importance of duties, chores, responsibilities, and rules appeal to their children on this stage. Church leaders who emphasize the ten commandments, the laws of the church and obedience to the pope appeal to this stage.

Level Three: Post-Conventional Morality

STAGE FIVE: THE SOCIAL CONTRACT

Stage five maintains loyalty to the system and its rules, but recognizes that such rules derive their power from the people and are meant to serve the people. Therefore, laws can be changed and there can be exceptions to the rule. The stage five person is more flexible in his or her understanding of the law and the system and works from within the system to change it. The Constitution of the United States is similar to stage five reasoning in that its authors allowed for it to be amended. Parents who allow their children a voice in establishing rules appeal to them on this stage. Church leaders who evoke the insight and wisdom of the entire church act from this level.

STAGE SIX: UNIVERSAL PRINCIPLES

The final and most mature stage of moral reasoning, according to Kohlberg, is the person who acts out of universal principles that he or she has personally appropriated into his or her life. These principles are universally and transculturally valid. The person operating at this stage is willing to challenge the system itself if necessary. For Kohlberg, the principles of justice and human rights and dignity are the highest of the universal principles. Parents who live these values by example appeal to their children at this level. Church leaders who take prophetic stands on the rights and dignity of all men and women are acting on this level. Certainly much of the teaching and deeds of Christ would be on level six.

According to Kohlberg, each stage leads to the next. The best way to help a person advance in moral reasoning is to discover his or her basic stage and appeal one stage higher. He also believes that people are not consistent in their moral reasoning and that only a small minority of adults are consistently reasoning on the third level (stages five or six).

While Kohlberg's findings need to be continually scrutinized and reevaluated, they do offer an interesting insight into the notion of conscience. They profoundly affirm the insight of the natural law which believes that there are universal principles to which all men and women are drawn. These principles, according to both natural law and Kohlberg, are transcultural.

In addition, Kohlberg's research can help explain much of the ambiguity concerning the notion of conscience in the church. There are many people (including church leaders) who shy away from the expression "Follow your conscience." Kohlberg's stages indicate why caution is not always a bad idea. People operating at different levels of moral development will "hear" different things when they hear "Follow your conscience."

Level One (stages one and two) will hear that there is no punishment or reward for their behavior. In essence, there is no authority to back up any rules or laws; therefore I can do whatever I want. "Follow your conscience" at this level becomes a code phrase for license, doing whatever one feels like without regard to the consequences.

Level Two (stages three and four) will often panic when told to follow their conscience. They depend highly on the expectations of others in order to make decisions. They feel insecure when expectations and laws are removed. Thus, for many Catholics the period following the Second Vatican Council was anxiety-producing because it was no longer so clear what constituted a "good Catholic." Following conscience meant following the laws of the church, and now many were being taken away. The same holds true for children. They need rules and expectations, and if they are given too much freedom too quickly, it tends to be more harmful than helpful.

Level Three (stages five and six) will truly understand the meaning of conscience. They know that "follow your conscience" means "do what is right, to work for the good of others, to love, to seek justice, to act honestly." Thus, from a Christian perspective, it is on stages five and six that conscience finds its true meaning. A person who chooses to go against commonly accepted standards of right and wrong in order to follow his or her conscience does so not for convenience but out of a sense of love or justice or truth.

Conscience: The Whole Person

From what we have seen thus far, it is fair to say that conscience is not something that one *has* as much as it is something that one *is*. It is in no way an addendum to my self. It is me insofar as my values, choices, attitudes and history determine who I am as a human person. The formation of Christian conscience then is not limited to instructing the mind with right information. It is enabling the whole person to grow and develop in his or her relationship to self, others and God. Fr. Bernard Häring describes it this way:

> Being created for wholeness, we can dynamically decipher and experience the good to which God calls us in the particular situation. One's conscience is healthy only when the whole person—the emotional as well as the intellectual elements and energies of the will—is functioning in a profound har-

29

mony in the depths of one's being. . . . Conscience has to do with man's total selfhood as a moral agent. The intellectual, volitional and emotional dynamics are not separated: they mutually compenetrate in the very depth where the person is person to himself.[2]

Summary

1. In order to understand the psychological basis for conscience, Freud's distinction of id, ego and superego is very helpful.
2. The id is the instinctual drive for pleasure; the superego is the internalized rules of authority, especially of one's parents; the ego is the principle of self-direction and self-appropriation.
3. Freud identified conscience with superego but it is more properly identified with ego strength.
4. The stronger the ego, the greater a person will be self-directed rather than driven by the sub-conscious compulsion of the id or the external prohibitions of the superego.
5. John Glaser distinguishes several critical distinctions between superego and conscience. Key to them is the freedom of the conscience to love and the superego's submission to external laws and authority.
6. Jean Piaget studied moral judgment in children and distinguished between two fundamental stages. Heteronomous moral judgments are based on authority, rules and material consequences. Autonomous moral judgments understand the rules in the context of social interaction and relationships.
7. Lawrence Kohlberg distinguished six stages of moral reasoning. These stages progress from punishment/reward orientation to a concern for the estimation of others and the law and finally an appreciation of the values and principles of conscience.

Questions for Review

1. Define id, ego and superego.
2. What are some of the essential differences between superego and conscience?
3. Explain Piaget's stages of heteronomy and autonomy. How would you relate them to superego and conscience?
4. Describe Kohlberg's six stages of moral reasoning.
5. How does Kohlberg's theory relate to the notion of superego and conscience? How does it relate to natural law theory?

For Personal Reflection and Discussion

1. Draw a time line of your life. Mark on the line the key choices that you have made that helped shape who you are as a person.

2. Susan is sweet sixteen and pregnant. She is contemplating an abortion. List *one reason* for each of Kohlberg's stages why she might or might not choose the abortion. (Example: stage one: "If my dad finds out I'm pregnant, he will kill me.")

3. To what extent is your life directed by the superego? Give examples. Who and what are the powerful superego influences in your life? What decisions have you made that really reflect your conscience?

Suggested Reading

Duska, Ronald and Mariellen Whelan. *Moral Development: A Guide to Piaget and Kohlberg.* New York/Paramus/Toronto: Paulist Press, 1975.

Nelson, C. Ellis. *Conscience: Theological and Psychological Perspectives.* New York/Paramus/Toronto: Newman Press, 1973.

3

Sin, Virtue and Freedom

I entered high school just as the Second Vatican Council was about to come to a close. Its effects had yet to be felt deeply in the church and certainly were not apparent in the text that we used concerning sexuality. In the book were catalogued virtually every sexual thought and deed (with very creative euphemisms to describe them) and a corresponding sin, either mortal or venial. Thus, sexual thoughts were subdivided into those that occurred without volition and those that were allowed to become full-blown fantasies. The former were not sinful at all; the latter were mortally sinful. Likewise, kissing was subdivided into numerous categories that were either not sinful, or venially sinful, or mortally sinful. (It seemed terribly unfair to me that sexual thoughts or kisses could be on the same level of sinfulness as sexual intercourse. In the mind of a fourteen year old, if you were going to commit a mortal sin, why not go all the way?)

Our interest here is not so much sexual morality as it is the very understanding of sin at work. The lines were very clearly drawn, and right and wrong were easily understood. The word conscience was not mentioned. Today one sometimes hears the lament that sin has disappeared from the preaching and the teaching of the church. One thing is certain: the theology or explanation of sin has certainly undergone tremendous renewal. In this chapter we will briefly look at the basic outline for an understanding of sin today.

Biblical Understanding of Sin

The Hebrew Scriptures

In the story of Adam and Eve in the book of Genesis, we see the biblical author trying to come to grips with the essential mystery of human iniquity: If God is all good and his creation is good, where has evil come from? Why do human beings hurt and destroy one another? In the story of Adam and Eve, the tree and the fruit and the serpent, the author is saying that it was human beings who chose to disobey God. Sin is the result of human choices. Because of their choice, Adam and Eve have destroyed the paradisal existence that God intended for them. Sin thwarts and perverts our true human happiness.

Because of the sins of men and women, human beings are in a "state of sin" and in need of salvation. God, however, does not abandon sinful humankind but offers to the people of Israel a covenant, a relationship based on mutual fidelity. It was the exodus, with Moses leading the Jews from slavery in Egypt, that was the crucial experience of the people of Israel. Through Moses, God offered his covenant which was based on his law. It was through fidelity to the law of God that the Jews attained righteousness. The author of the first psalm captures the Jewish insight into the two paths of life—the way of the sinner and the way of the just:

> Happy the man who follows not the counsel of the
> wicked
> Nor walks in the way of sinners, nor sits in the com-
> pany of the insolent,
> But delights in the law of the Lord and meditates on
> his law day and night.
> He is like a tree planted near running water,
> That yields its fruit in due season, and whose leaves
> never fade.
> (Whatever he does, prospers.)

33

Not so the wicked, not so.
They are like chaff which the wind drives away.
Therefore in judgment the wicked shall not stand,
Nor shall sinners, in the assembly of the just.
For the Lord watches over the way of the just but the
way of the wicked vanishes.

To violate the torah, God's law and teaching, was to
break faith with God. There was more at stake than simple
obedience: the covenant was essentially relational.

The prophets of Israel and Judea often emphasized the
need to go beyond the ritual requirements of the law and to
care for the poor and the oppressed. The prophet Isaiah criticized the fasting of the righteous: "This, rather, is the fasting
that I seek: releasing those bound unjustly, untying the thongs
of the yoke; sharing your bread with the hungry" (Is 58:6–7).
Simple obedience to the law did not take one far enough into
the mystery of God's love. Sin resides not only in disobedi-
ence but more profoundly in the heart. Thus the prophet
Jeremiah speaks of a day when the law shall be written in the
hearts of the people:

The days are coming, says the Lord, when I will
make a new covenant with the house of Israel and
the house of Judah. . . . I will place my law within
them and write it upon their hearts; I will be their
God and they shall be my people (Jer 31:31–33).

The Hebrew scriptures often refer to sin as idolatry. It is
a failure to place God above all else.

The New Testament

One of the principal insights into the nature of sin in the
gospels can be found in Jesus' nickname: "friend of sinners."
Jesus' call to repentance and conversion assumes that human
beings are sinners in need of God's mercy and grace. His

message was "good news" for sinners. It was a message about the Father's love for sinful mankind. Yet there was no complacency in the call of Jesus. Like the prophets of the Old Testament, Jesus called the people to a love that revealed itself in action. He condemned those who saw themselves as "righteous" and looked down upon sinners. Like the prophets, Jesus emphasized the human heart as the wellspring of both love and sin. Jesus spoke much more about love than about sin. From those teachings we can draw conclusions about the nature of sin. If the greatest of the commandments was to love God and other people, then sin was primarily a failure to love God with all one's heart and to love others.

For Paul, the great theologian of the New Testament, sin is usually described in the context of the human state of being (what we would call original sin or human sinfulness, in general). All things must be placed in the new light of Christ's redemption, and thus sin is perceived as that power that prevailed in the world until the great Christ event. Paul contrasts Christ with Adam. Adam represents "fallen" human beings, those trapped by the power of sin. Christ represents the new man, the one who is faithful to God and who brings grace and life.

Original Sin and the Need for Conversion

In order to reflect on our own experience of the meaning of sin, we shall begin not with doctrine, laws, commandments, or theology. We begin with common human experience. Read the newspaper today. Something is terribly wrong with the world that we live in. It is plagued with violence, deceit, power-seeking, sexual abuse of all kinds, anger, hatred, bigotry, cynicism and apathy. But look again. The world is filled with human warmth and affection, friendship, courage, love, service and self-sacrifice. This is a schizophrenic planet, and mother earth's children are divided. They have a great capacity for love and a capacity for betrayal as well. If we move more deeply into our experience of life, we may recognize that "we" are "they." We are graced, given life and love as a gift. We love in return. Yet we fail to love. We betray our own best selves, sometimes tragically so.

This state of social and personal brokenness is what is theologically called *original sin*. It is one of the most misunderstood doctrines in the church. Most often it seems associated with babies and baptism, but it is meant to explain the reality of the human condition as we know it. What is that reality? We find it in Jesus' fundamental proclamation: "Change your lives! The reign of God is at hand!" The good news begins with a call to repentance, to conversion. Human beings are in need of a fundamental change of perspective. They do not see and love as God sees and loves. We must change our hearts if we are to uncover our true destiny both personally and communally. Original sin is not a sin that we commit, or that we choose. It is one that we are "born into" in two ways. First, all humans have an inclination to selfishness, a pre-disposition to choose the easy and the convenient before the good and the loving. This inclination is not chosen. It is a part of our humanity. St. Paul describes it this way: "I cannot even understand my own actions. I do not do what I want to do but what I hate" (Rom 7:15). Theologian John Shea describes it nicely: "The mystery of human iniquity is that we seek to kill the love that saves us." This inclination co-exists with a powerful capacity to know and do the good—to love. Second, humans are born into a sinful (and graced) world. The world communicates love and truth but also hatred and deceit. We "inherit" not only the love, affection and truth of those who love us but also the false presumptions and the disvalues of the world that we are born into. When we baptize an infant (or an adult), we believe that it "removes" original sin in the sense that it gives the person a different orientation. It offers the person a new way of living and being. It unmasks the reality of sin with the reality of God's grace and with the promise of the community to support this person in the way of the Spirit and against the lies of sin and evil.

Original sin then is the "web of sin" that we are born into and can possibly be caught up in. This sinful situation cries out for liberation, freedom, and salvation. It is precisely that which Christians believe God has offered in Jesus Christ. There is a "way out" for the human race. There exists original grace as well as original sin. God does not start to love us at baptism, as if water and sacrament change God's disposition. Rather, his love is an abiding condition of our being. Baptism is for our benefit, not God's. It is to initiate us into the community that strives to live in the spirit of Jesus Christ. God's offer of love draws us toward the infinite mystery of love. To be human is by definition to be related to God and drawn to God's love. This is done in human freedom when we choose to love other people. For God is never loved directly as an object of our experience, but is loved in and through our love for others as both the source and the ultimate goal of that love.

The Fundamental Option

This dynamism of our being toward God as the infinite mystery of life and love has been termed the "supernatural existential" by Karl Rahner. According to Rahner this dimension of our lives is precisely what makes us human. It is "supernatural" because it is oriented toward God. There is no human completion to the drive. It is a never-ending openness to move more deeply into the mystery of love and truth. Put simply, in this life one never fully arrives. It is an "existential" in that it is an in-built dynamism of our being. Like a receptor made to pick up sound waves for a radio, we are "built" with an openness to God as infinite love and truth. However, our attraction to God is not automatic. It must be activated. We must decide; we must say "yes." It is the human capacity for decision and self-determination that enables us to both love and refuse to love. It is on the level of decision that we discover the capacity for *personal sin*.

Core human freedom is the freedom to say yes or no to

the fundamental direction of our lives as a movement in love of others and God. Moral theologians call this decision a *fundamental option*. The fundamental option is the most basic decision that we make about ourselves as persons. It establishes the ultimate direction of our lives: either as a life committed in love to others or one that is essentially self-centered and rejects the demands of love. Most theologians today describe *mortal sin* as a rejection of the basic decision to be a person committed to love. The fundamental option is one that is oriented toward the self. Such a decision is very difficult to determine. It resides in the heart and is not always discernible from outer appearances. Such a sin is mortal because it literally kills. It does not lead to life but to loneliness, separation from the human community, God and our true selves. Mortal sin is not necessarily irreversible. It is certainly possible to change the direction of one's being. But it would be rare, if not impossible, to find a person changing his or her fundamental option frequently.

Venial sins are those failures to love that do not involve our core freedom. They are not basic decisions to change the direction of our lives. They are, rather, failures to be faithful to that basic decision which has not changed.

In the past, mortal sins were often judged by the seriousness of the offense. Contemporary theologians put more emphasis on the amount of personal involvement than on the nature of the offense. This is not to say that serious sins are not serious. They are, but they are not necessarily mortal. Let's look at an example:

Mr. Smith is in business. Things have not been going well, and he has been under a great deal of professional strain. On the home front, he and Mrs. Smith have not had the kind of time they need together and communication has suffered. The baby has had them both up at night, and they are both under stress. On a business trip, Mr. Smith has a couple of drinks at dinner with some associates, meets a single woman, and winds up going to bed with her. Has Mr. Smith committed a mortal sin?

The best answer, of course, is: God knows. Only God judges the human heart. But we use the example to illustrate a point. It is possible that Mr. Smith has slowly been changing the basic choice of his life. This infidelity simply makes dramatic what has been happening less dramatically: Mr. Smith is more interested in himself than anyone else. If this is the case, then the sin may represent a fundamental option that is mortally sinful. On the other hand, this marital infidelity may be the jolt to help Mr. Smith recognize that his marriage and life are in need of conversion. It may be something that he regrets deeply because it is in fact contrary to his true option in life, which is one of love. In this case, the sin is very serious (it could do great damage to his marriage), but it is not mortal sin.

The Wrong Focus

For many, the theology of the fundamental option better explains the reality of mortal and venial sin. However, there is a danger that goes with it. It can be easy to lose sight of the fact that all sin is in some ways serious. Pre-occupation with the cataloguing of sins as mortal, venial or serious is the wrong focus. All sin is to be avoided. The attitude that something is *only* a venial sin (and therefore not very serious) is precisely the attitude that leads to mortal sin. It is a commitment to weakness. The focus for a mature conscience is never "What am I allowed to get away with?" but rather to discern the call of love more and more deeply.

Sins of Omission

Sin is often described as a failure to love, or a failure to choose what one knows to be the best course of action. It is commonly seen as something that we "do" wrong. Fair enough. But there is another dimension to sin that is often overlooked. These are sins of omission. The fact is that it is very possible to do nothing "wrong" and still commit very serious sins. Apathy, not caring, is among the deadliest of sins. Recall the parables that Jesus told of the good Samaritan (Lk 10) and the rich man and Lazarus (Lk 16). The "villains" of the stories did nothing wrong. But they failed to love when their love was needed. Sin is often an absence, an emptiness—nothing, where love should be.

Sin, Freedom and Maturity

If we recall what was said concerning conscience and psychology, it is apparent that not all evil actions committed by people are personally sinful. One's freedom may be grossly limited for emotional or mental reasons. One's personal maturity may limit personal culpability. What may truly be sinful for one person may not be for another.

Social Sin

Strictly speaking, sin is always a personal choice. However, we also speak of sin analogously when we speak of original sin and social sin. Social sin refers here not to individual acts committed but to the "sinful structures" within society that degrade and oppress human beings. These structures are always the result of human choices. Social sin is thus "institutionalized." It becomes part of the fabric of a society. It establishes false, unconscious presumptions in the minds of people who live within the confines of the institution. Racism, classism, materialism, militarism, consumerism, a disproportionate nationalism, and sexism are all examples of sins that have taken on a life of their own within the institutions of society. Pope John Paul II, in his encyclical *On Social Concern*, describes the military struggle between east and west and the economic struggle between north and south as examples of social sin that exploit the poor and prepare for war. As such, he writes:

A world divided into blocs, in which, instead of solidarity, imperialism and exploitation hold sway, can only be a world structured in sin.[1]

Sin and Virtue

If sin is an absence, then virtue is a plenitude, a fullness of being, the result of continued and consistent acts of love and goodness. Virtue is often referred to as a "habit," but it is not simply mindless repetition. It is a habit or way of being, so deeply ingrained that it has become a part of oneself. Likewise, sin is also "habitual" in that our lives often take on patterns of behavior and attitudes. In order to better understand the dynamics of sin and virtue, we will examine a classic list of sins, known as the capital or deadly sins. For each of the deadly sins we will examine a corresponding virtue:

1. a. *Pride.* In common usage, the word "pride" usually means two very different things. It has a positive, virtuous meaning: to take pride in one's self, meaning to possess sufficient self-respect. Pride, however, as one of the deadly sins, is considered the deadliest. In this sense, pride is the arrogance born of self-centeredness. The proud person places himself or herself at the center of the universe. As such, pride is a form of self-idolatry. It is an exaggerated sense of one's own importance which subordinates all else to its own needs. Pride seeks not the good of the other, but its own honor and exaltation. The proud person is the one truly cut off from God and others who exist only to serve him or her.

b. *Humility.* The proud person lacks the virtue and grace of humility. Humility is not a lack of self-respect as it is often portrayed. Above all else, humility is truth. It is the recognition and acceptance of one's humanity, with all its glory and limits. The word humility is derived from the Latin *humus*, meaning "of the earth." The humble person recognizes his or her creaturely status. He or she is not the center of the universe: God is. The humble person is able to accept all that has been given to him or her—intelligence, heart, soul, spirit, friends, family—with an attitude of praise and thanksgiving. The humble person does not deny his or her talents or abilities but recognizes their source and realizes that ultimately all praise belongs to God. The humble person is capable, as the proud person is not, of truly praising others and finding joy in their happiness.

2. a. *Envy.* Envy is more than simply wishing that one had the qualities that belong to another person. There is a natural desire to admire and emulate the strengths of others. Envy, as a sin, is a refusal to accept one's own limits (and strengths) and truly begrudges the virtues and gifts of another. It feels unduly wronged and cheated that another might have what it lacks. It often leads to bitterness and slander.

b. *Self-Acceptance.* The virtue of self-acceptance is not simply a bromide of pop psychology for happiness. It is rooted in the virtue of faith. In faith, one believes that God is loving Abba, Father. The root of our worth is in relationship to God as a beloved child. It is not the possession of certain attributes that gives our lives value. Our lives have value in themselves as children of God, as brothers and sisters to each other. Thus, self-acceptance means realizing the true source of human value. This certainly goes against the grain of life in the world which often measures our worth in terms of beauty, or intelligence, or charm, or financial success . . .

3. a. *Greed.* Greed is an inordinate desire for material possessions and wealth. This deadly sin is an affront to Jesus' call to prepare for the coming of God's kingdom, because the greedy person is interested only in one kingdom: his or her own. In countries where wealth abounds, there is a terrible temptation to measure one's value in terms of financial and material success. Materialism does more than anything to engender greed.

b. *Social Justice.* As we near the end of the second millennium, we have become more and more aware of our unity as a planet. We have become more sensitized to the reality of the global village. In a world where one billion people are either starving or malnourished, greed is more than ever a contradiction to the spirit of the gospel. The virtue of social justice recognizes that the goods of the earth are intended for all, and seeks to live in such a way that all are invited to share in the banquet of human solidarity. In particular, social justice recognizes that those who "have" must find ways to order society to include all those who "have not."

4. a. *Lust.* Early in his pontificate, Pope John Paul II gave a series of talks on the meaning of human sexuality. Despite the high quality of the talks, they were ignored by the secular press until he said that a husband should not lust after his wife. This seemed odd and humorous (and newsworthy), so the secular media printed the statement (usually out of context). The pope did not mean that a man should not be erotically attracted to his wife. He meant that a husband should never view his wife only as a sexual object. For that is the sin of lust (although it is rarely associated with married couples). Lust is the attitude of heart that sees in the other person the gratification of his or her sexual needs. It reduces the person to an object. As an habitual state of heart, lust destroys a person's capacity for intimacy and commitment, for it is never truly interested in the person.

b. *Chastity.* Chastity, on the other hand, understands the nature of sexual relationships very differently. Sex is primarily about loving, committed relationships, and it is the virtue of chastity that places the needs of genuine love above the needs for sexual gratification. Chastity realizes that an intimate, sexual relationship involves much more than biological or emotional needs. Fidelity and love mean more than simply limiting the number of sex partners to one. Fidelity means being faithful in communication, sacrifice, care, and mutuality. The chaste person is unwilling to ever "use" his or her partner. For the chaste person the meaning of sex is found in the context of mutually committed love.

43

5. a. *Anger.* To begin, there is a big difference between the feeling of anger and the sin of anger. It is possible that feeling angry is a very appropriate feeling (recall Jesus chasing the merchants from the temple). St. Augustine believed that we should feel angry in the face of injustice. If we did not, something was spiritually wrong. What then is the sin of anger? It is more akin to hatred than feeling angry. It is destructive passion against anything or anyone whom it sees as an enemy (real or perceived). Anger is most often born of impatience. It is self-indulgent and lacks the maturity needed for delayed gratification. Anger is usually disproportionate. It responds with more power than is in any way helpful. Very often it is displaced—it is launched against the nearest target but not the right one. Anger often leads to insults and abuse, both verbal and physical. It is incapable of accepting the limits of others. In its psychological roots, the angry person is often the one who had been abused and hurt by others.

b. *Patience.* If anger cannot accept the limits of others, patience is schooled in the art of unconditional love. The patient person is much more at peace with his or her own limitations, and realizes that all human beings are still in process. The patient person is more able to wait, to postpone gratification, to suffer the weaknesses of others (the word "patience" comes from the Latin word meaning to suffer). Perhaps more than anything else, the patient person knows how to laugh.

6. a. *Gluttony.* Gluttony is self-indulgence in the area of food, drink or drugs. It is similar to lust in that it treats the body as a pleasure machine rather than Paul's insight that it is a temple of the Holy Spirit. The gluttonous person abuses rather than uses. At the heart of this sin is the failure to recognize the importance and dignity of the human body.

b. *Self-Respect.* For Christians, the body is not something that simply houses the soul. It is an essential part of one's very self. Respect for one's body involves discipline, moderation, prudence, exercise, good eating habits. At the

44

heart of this virtue is St. Francis' recognition that all creation is brother or sister to us. We are creatures, therefore bodily. To love ourselves we must respect our bodies.

7. a. *Sloth.* Sloth is not simply laziness, but more specifically a lack of commitment to the spiritual good. Sloth may do nothing "wrong" but it does nothing at all in the spiritual life. Thus it abandons the need for prayer, spiritual reading, the sacraments, commitments to the poor, to fellowship in the church. Sloth is the smallness of heart that seeks its own ease above the love of God and neighbor.

b. *Love.* The command cited by Jesus as the greatest points to the dynamic, passionate, creative dimension of living and loving: we are to love God with all our heart, mind, soul and strength. Love is energy directed for the good of the other. It is praise and worship and fidelity to God. Love is what sanctifies us, and it is anything but "boring." It is an impassioned response to love of God. It is the opposite of sloth: it cares.

Sin and Grace

We have been trying to get a handle on the mystery of sin. In order to do so, we have looked briefly at some biblical insights, human experience, contemporary moral theology, and the traditional deadly sins and their accompanying virtues. Yet sin somehow manages to defy our attempts to systematize it. The reason for this, I believe, is because sin cannot be understood without grace. Sin can easily be understood as human limitations, psychological compulsions, immaturity, social determinism, etc. It is only when grace appears on the subject that sin can be seen as sin, because grace reveals the true nature of sin, as the absence of divine love. One who has never seen the light has no way to truly understand and explain the darkness all around. It is for this reason that the greatest saints describe themselves as the greatest sinners. This is not false humility. This is simply the voices of those who know the brightness of the light. It is for this reason that a "sense of sin" is a sign of the life of the Spirit in the church. Eugene Kennedy has described the situation:

> This consciousness of our sinful condition does not drape the soul in black bunting as much as it attunes it to the unretouched reality of our existence. It is best heard in those who strive to live by the Spirit. It lives also in ancient rituals and practices through which human sinfulness is acknowledged, almost embraced, and dealt with straightforwardly. . . . Allowing for the distortion of guilt that has undergirded the catholic conflict, the sense of sin, at its base, remains a reliable insight into the way the world works and the way people meet and relate to each other.[2]

Summary

1. In the Hebrew scriptures, sin is a violation of the covenant relationship with God. For the prophets, the focus was often on social sins against the needs of the poor and the oppressed.
2. Jesus was known as the "friend of sinners." He preached a gospel of mercy and called sinners to repentance.
3. Paul emphasized the freedom from sin that Christ had brought to those who believed in him.
4. Original sin is not one that we commit. It is rather a description of the human situation: beings who are inclined to selfishness and who live in a world of sin.
5. Personal sin is the individual human decision that is always in some way a failure and refusal to love.
6. Theologians use the term "fundamental option" to describe the most basic choice and direction of a person's life, either in openness to love or turned in on oneself.

7. Mortal sin is often described as the fundamental option for self. It emphasizes the depth of the personal choice more than any individual act.
8. Venial sins are those committed by fundamentally loving people. They are a betrayal but not a reversal of one's true orientation.
9. Sins of omission are those acts of love that we fail to perform even though we do nothing wrong.
10. The seven deadly sins are signs of a life turned away from love of God and others.
11. Virtue is a "habit of being," an ingrained, positive response of one's self to the challenge of human values.
12. Sin is only recognizable as sin through the eyes of faith and with the aid of grace.

Questions for Review

1. What are some of the key biblical insights into the nature of sin?
2. How is original sin a term that is descriptive of ourselves and the world we live in?
3. What is meant by the fundamental option?
4. Describe personal, mortal, venial and social sin.
5. What is a virtue?
6. What are the seven deadly sins?

For Personal Reflection and Discussion

1. Using newspapers and magazines, make a list of ways in which the world is "structured in sin."

2. Write a contemporary examination of conscience.

3. Research the original meanings of the ten commandments. How do the principles of these commandments continue to apply today?

Suggested Reading

Kennedy, Eugene. *A Sense of Life, A Sense of Sin.* Garden City: Image Books, 1975.

Menninger, Karl. *Whatever Became of Sin?* New York: Hawthorn Books, 1973.

4

The Message and Life of Jesus: A New Way of Seeing and Living

In this chapter, we begin to look at that which makes Christian conscience distinctively Christian: the person and teaching of Christ. In the first chapter we spoke of the need for conscience to be informed and formed. Conscience does not simply activate itself on its own without guidance. For Christians, the gospels play a uniquely important role in the formation and development of conscience. By no means do they provide the only source for conscience formation, but they are truly foundational. Anything that is constructed and built must somehow be built upon them.

According to the four gospels, Jesus never once used the word "conscience" or the expression "Follow your conscience." When people asked him how they should live, Jesus was not so wishy-washy as to say, "Do whatever you think is best." Jesus was very clear and certain about his ideas concerning the moral life. However, scripture scholars agree that Jesus' goal or mission in life was not to give people new commandments or simply instruct them what to do. Jesus was not a moral theologian, and he did not have a systematic approach to right and wrong. Instead Jesus taught and preached about the "coming of the reign of God." This message had profound implications for living. He called people to "conversion" or "metanoia." This was not only a change of heart but a whole new way of seeing reality from God's perspective. For Jesus, morality was inseparable from spirituality. For him, what we *do* must be rooted in our understanding of ourselves in relation to God and others. For Jesus, morality is rooted in relationship. Morality is not extrinsic rules from God but the living out of our true humanity as sons and daughters of God. In this chapter I would like to try to systematize and summarize some of the highlights of Jesus' vision that form the foundation for a Christian understanding of morality and conscience.

1. *Abba.* If we were forced to narrow the message of Jesus to one word, this would be the one. The word "Abba" is an Aramaic word used by Jesus to describe God. It means "dad" or "daddy." It was a term of familiarity and love and affection used by a child (young or old) for his or her father. This word grounds Jesus' own spirituality and our relationship to each other. If we are all sons and daughters of a loving Abba, Father, then life can no longer be lived the same way. If we see life from this perspective, if we learn how to *feel* the truth of this word, then we learn much about the perspective of Jesus himself. We begin to see why he was the way he was: open, forgiving, caring, reaching out to the lost and the forgotten, angry with the powers that oppressed the people. It is all rooted in the one word: Abba. The Lord of the universe is the loving Father of all, and we are brothers and sisters to each other.

2. *The Reign of God.* At the heart of the teaching and the message of Jesus is the coming of the reign of God. The first words from his mouth in the gospel of Mark declare the coming of the reign: "Now is the time of fulfillment. The reign of God is at hand. Reform your lives and believe in the gospel." For Jesus, the coming of God's reign marked a new era in the world in which the lordship and power of God was at work. Again, Jesus offers no systematic theology of the reign of God. Instead he offers parables and stories that describe the

reign. From these parables we can discern the following characteristics of God's reign.

a. *God's Reign or Kingdom Is the Power of God at Work.* Bringing about the reign of God is ultimately not a human task but the work of God. Jesus presents an image of the world in which God is powerfully at work doing more than people can hope or imagine. The extraordinary power of God is the subject of two well-known but short parables.

"The reign of God is like a mustard seed which someone took and sowed in his field. It is the smallest seed of all, yet when full-grown it is the largest of plants. It becomes so big a shrub that the birds of the sky come and build their nests in its branches." He offered still another image: "The reign of God is like yeast which a woman took and kneaded into three measures of flour. Eventually the whole mass of dough began to rise" (Mt 13:31–33).

In these parables the emphasis is on the extraordinary transformation that takes place within the dough and through the mustard seed. They emphasize the power of God at work. The spiritual and moral life, then, is a cooperation with this power at work. If we were to read only these parables, it might lead to a sense of quietism: the belief that all is in God's hands and that we need do nothing. It is impossible to believe this, however, in light of the other teachings of Jesus.

b. *God's Reign Demands a Response on Our Part*

"The reign of God is like a buried treasure which a man found in a field. He hid it again and, rejoicing at his find, went and sold all that he had and bought that field. Or again the kingdom of heaven is like a merchant's search for fine pearls. When he found one really valuable pearl, he went back and put up for sale all that he had and bought it" (Mt 13:44–46).

In the parables of the treasure and of the pearl, the key point is on the response of those who find something of great value. God's reign demands a response from us. Like the merchant, we must be willing to make the complete commitment. But it is also a commitment that leads to joy and rejoicing. It is not asceticism for its own sake: it is commitment for the sake of God's reign. They are parables that challenge us to look at our response to God's offer. Whose kingdom are we busy building: God's or our own?

c. *The Reign of God Is Both a Present and a Future Reality.* In the history of Christianity, there has been a tendency at times to emphasize that "heaven" or the reign of God is a future reality. There is much truth in this. But it also misses much of Jesus' insistence that God's reign is at work now, if incompletely. His parables of "judgment" emphasize the relationship between the present order and the future.

"The reign of God may be likened to a man who sowed good seed in his field. While everyone was asleep, his enemy came and sowed weeds through the wheat and made off. When the crop began to mature and yield grain, the weeds made their appearance as well. The owner's slaves came to him and said, 'Sir, did you not sow good seed in your field? Where are the weeds coming from?' He said, 'I see an enemy's hand in this.' His slaves said to him, 'Do you want us to go out and pull them up?' 'No,' he replied, 'pull up the weeds and you might take the wheat along with them. Let them grow together until harvest; then at harvest time I will order the harvesters, First collect the weeds and bundle them up to burn, then gather the wheat into my barn' " (Mt 13:24–30).

The parable represents the situation of good and evil in the world. It reminds us that the question of good and evil is one that will ultimately be decided by God, and that our decisions have ultimate consequences.

3. *Love of God and Love of Others Is Inseparable.* Jesus was recognized as a rabbi (teacher) by the people of his time and was often addressed by that title. Typically, they would ask him from time to time which of the laws of the torah were the most important. On one occasion the Pharisees were trying to trap him when they asked the question:

" 'Teacher, which commandment of the law is the greatest?' Jesus said to him: 'You shall love the Lord your God with your whole heart, with your whole soul and with all your mind. This is the greatest and the first commandment. The second is like it: You shall love your neighbor as yourself' " (Mt 22:36– 39).

There is nothing surprising about Jesus' choice of the greatest of the commandments (Deut 6:5). It would have been chosen by many rabbis. What was unique about Jesus was his insistence on tying the second commandment (Lev 19:18) to the first. While it was unique, it was also absolutely consistent with everything Jesus ever said or did. In the gospels, love for God and love for other people are absolutely inseparable realities. Long after the death of Jesus, John spells this out clearly in one of his letters in the New Testament: "If anyone says, 'My love is fixed on God,' but hates his brother, he is a liar. One who has no love for the brother he has seen cannot love the God he has not seen" (1 Jn 4:20).

4. *Love Has No Boundaries.* On one occasion, a scribe (an expert in the torah) asked Jesus to explain the meaning of the commandment from Leviticus to love one's neighbor as oneself. Jesus replied with the famous story of the good Samaritan. The meaning of the parable is easily lost on us today. Its apparent meaning is to help those in need. But there was much more to it when Jesus originally told the story. It was told in response to the question: "Who is my neighbor?" In the story Jesus tells of two "good guys," a Levite and a priest, who pass by the man in the ditch. But a Samaritan stops to help, takes him to an inn and pays for his expenses. Samaritans and Jews hated each other. They were the Hatfields and McCoys of Palestine two thousand years ago. But Jesus has answered the question. Who is my neighbor that I must love? Even my most hated enemy. In the sermon on the mount he put it this way:

"You have heard the commandment, 'You shall love your countryman but hate your enemy.' My command to you is: love your enemies and pray for your persecutors. This will prove that you are sons of your heavenly Father, for his sun rises on the bad and the good, he rains on the just and the unjust. If you love those who love you, what merit is there in that? Do not tax collectors do as much? In a word, you must be made perfect, even as your heavenly Father is perfect" (Mt 5:43–48).

5. *Forgiveness.* Jesus' message was loaded with paradoxes. We have just read how he exhorted his followers to "be made perfect," and yet it is doubtful that any man ever lived who had a deeper feeling for human weakness than did Jesus. As much as any other virtue, forgiveness rings through the gospel like "the good news" it claimed to be. At the heart of Jesus' message was God's love for sinful people, those who were not yet made perfect. In fact, Jesus' association

with sinners often got him into hot water with the religious leaders of his time:

> While Jesus was reclining to eat in Levi's house, many tax collectors and those known to as sinners joined him and his disciples at dinner. The number of those who followed him was large. When the scribes who belonged to the Pharisee party saw that he was eating with tax collectors and offenders against the law, they complained to his disciples, "Why does he eat with such as these?" Overhearing the remark, Jesus said to them, "People who are healthy do not need a doctor; sick people do. I have come to call sinners, not the self-righteous" (Mk 2:15–17).

Jesus' interest in sinners stems from his belief that all are sinners in need of God's mercy. Those who were "self-righteous" were missing the point. They believed that they were a different category of human being. There were the "sinners" and the righteous, and they were the righteous. For Jesus, there were sinners, some in much worse shape than others, but all sinners in need of God's mercy. (Even more profoundly, all are God's sons and daughters, no matter what they have done.)

6. *Compassion.* One of the compelling dimensions of Jesus' words and deeds is his compassion for those who are on the fringes of society. In the beginning of the gospel of Luke, Jesus identifies himself with the words of the prophet Isaiah as one who has come for the poor, the prisoner and the outcast:

> When the book of the prophet Isaiah was handed him, he unrolled the scroll and found the passage where it was written: "The spirit of the Lord is upon me; therefore he has anointed me. He has sent me

to bring glad tidings to the poor, to proclaim liberty to captives, recovery of sight to the blind and release to prisoners, to announce a year of favor from the Lord" (Lk 4:17–19).

Throughout his ministry Jesus shows concern for the least of his brothers and sisters. He reaches out to women, heals lepers and the sick, gives hope to the grieving. He goes so far as to instruct his disciples that "whatever you do for the least of my brothers and sisters, you do for me" (Mt 25:40). In that passage, Jesus says that ultimately our judgment will rest on how we have treated the least in society. He also makes this point in one of his parables:

> "Once there was a rich man who dressed in purple and linen and feasted splendidly every day. At his gate lay a beggar named Lazarus who was covered with sores. Lazarus longed to eat the scraps that fell from the rich man's table. The dogs even came and licked his sores. Eventually the beggar died. He was carried by angels to the bosom of Abraham. The rich man likewise died and was buried. From the abode of the dead where he was in torment, he raised his eyes and saw Abraham afar off, and Lazarus resting in his bosom.
> "He called out, 'Father Abraham, have pity on me. Send Lazarus to dip the tip of his finger in water to refresh my tongue, for I am tortured in these flames.' 'My child,' replied Abraham, 'remember that you were well off in your lifetime, while Lazarus was in misery. Now he has found consolation here, but you have found torment' " (Lk 16:19–25).

It is interesting to note in the story that, in traditional terms, the rich man has done nothing wrong. He did not cause Lazarus' poverty. He did not chase him from his gate or treat him rudely. He simply neglected him. He was without compassion for the poor man in need. It is very possible that after a while he simply did not see him anymore. When Pope John Paul II first visited America, he chose this parable to be the gospel for his mass at Yankee Stadium, and the reason was obvious. The United States runs the same temptation as the rich man in the story: to lose sight of the countless poor who lie starving outside our gate.

7. *Actions Speak Louder Than Words*. One of the problems that Christ encountered was the religious leadership of some of the scribes and Pharisees who knew the law and obeyed it but did not respond to the challenges of love. For Jesus their faith was mere show, a way of winning the approval of men but not of God. It matters little what we profess unless we put our words into deeds:

> "What do you think of this case? There was a man who had two sons. He approached the elder and said, 'Son go out and work in the vineyard today.' The son replied, 'I am on my way, sir'; but he never went. Then the man came to his second son and said the same thing. This son said in reply, 'No, I will not'; but afterward he regretted it and went. Which of the two did what the father wanted?" (Mt 21:28–31).

> "Anyone who hears my words and puts them into practice is like the wise man who built his house on rock. When the rainy season set in, the torrents came and the winds blew and buffeted his house. It did not collapse; it has been solidly set on rock" (Mt 7:24–25).

Later, the author of the letter of James would put it this way:

If a brother or sister has nothing to wear and no food for the day, and you say to them, "Goodbye and good luck! Keep warm and well fed," but do not meet their bodily needs, what good is that? So it is with the faith that does nothing in practice. It is thoroughly lifeless (Jas 2:15–17).

8. *Love's Roots Are in the Heart.* As much as Jesus emphasized actions over words, he also stressed the importance of the inner source of our deeds: the heart. He called not simply for a change of behavior, but for a change of heart as well. Perhaps this is seen most clearly in the sermon on the mount (Mt 5–7), in which Jesus implores his listeners to go beyond the demands of the torah:

"You have heard the commandment imposed by your forefathers, 'You shall not commit murder; every murderer shall be liable to judgment.' What I say to you is: everyone who grows angry with his brother shall be liable to judgment. . . .
"You have heard the commandment, 'You shall not commit adultery.' What I say to you is: anyone who looks lustfully at a woman has already committed adultery with her in his thoughts" (Mt 5:21–22, 27–28).

9. *A Spirit of Non-Violence and Moral Courage.* It is not uncommon to find a perception of Jesus that portrays him as being the first Boy Scout: courteous, kind, loving, giving. There is sometimes a milk & toast quality that people associate with Jesus which forgets that this man was beaten, crucified and killed. Jesus had two remarkable qualities that are hard to find in the same person: he had extraordinary moral courage and he lived that courage in a spirit of non-violence. He directly challenged the religious authorities who sought to control others by using the law as a weapon. In one scene

from the gospels, Jesus directly and arrogantly defied those who controlled the synagogues:

> He returned to the synagogue where there was a man whose hand was shriveled up. They kept an eye on Jesus to see if he would heal on the sabbath, hoping to be able to bring an accusation against him. He addressed the man with the shriveled hand: "Stand up here in front!" Then he said to them: "Is it permitted to do a good deed on the sabbath—or an evil one? To preserve life or to destroy it?" At this they remained silent. He looked around at them with anger, for he was deeply grieved that they had closed their minds against him. Then he said to the man, "Stretch out your hand." The man did so and his hand was perfectly restored (Mk 3:1–5).

Jesus defiantly broke one of the laws of the torah in front of the religious leaders to make a point: people are more important than rules, or in the words of Jesus, "The sabbath was made for man, not man for the sabbath" (Mk 2:27).

The Sadducees were the priests in Jerusalem who had control of the temple and its worship. At the time of Jesus, many of them were more interested in profits than in God, and once again Jesus was not afraid to challenge the powers:

> As the Jewish Passover was near, Jesus went up to Jerusalem. In the temple precincts he came upon people engaged in selling oxen, sheep and doves, and others seated changing coins. He made a whip of cords and drove sheep and oxen alike out of the temple area, and knocked over the money-changers' tables, spilling their coins. He told those who were selling doves: "Get them out of here!

Stop turning my Father's house into a marketplace" (Jn 2:13–16).

Jesus' confrontation with the Jewish authorities made him a threat to their authority. Likewise, the Romans were convinced that Jesus was no good for the public welfare and thus his courage led to his death. Throughout his ministry Jesus had rejected all appeals to become a political or military leader, and he would resist this last temptation once again. In the garden of Gethsemane, as he was being placed under arrest, one of his followers tried to defend Jesus. His response was: "Put back your sword where it belongs. Those who use the sword are sooner or later destroyed by it." In the end, Jesus lived the words that he had spoken:

"You have heard the commandment, 'An eye for an eye and a tooth for a tooth.' But what I say to you is: offer no resistance to injury. When a person strikes you on the right cheek, turn and offer him the other" (Mt 5:38–39).

10. *Radical Trust in God.* Is it really possible to live the way that Jesus offers—forgiveness, love of enemies, attentiveness to the poor, non-violence? These seem to be the stuff of which saints are made. What about ordinary human beings? Can they live this way? The gospels seem to indicate that ordinary human beings are the best candidates to live this way. They are the ones to whom Jesus seems most drawn in choosing his disciples. Many of them were fishermen. Jesus himself was a carpenter. They came with no special credentials. There does seem, however, to be one attribute that is necessary: radical trust in God. We see this most evident in the life of Jesus himself. This "way" that Jesus offers, this vision that he sets forth, does not come with promises of success or guarantees for happiness in this world. For Jesus, the words that he teaches his disciples to pray are the ones that he prays on the night before his death: "Thy will be

done." Ultimately our lives are in God's hands. The vision of Jesus calls for us to let go:

> "Stop worrying, then, over questions like, 'What are we to eat, or what are we to drink, or what are we to wear?' The unbelievers are always running after these things. Your heavenly Father knows all that you need. Seek first his kingship over you, his way of holiness, and all these things will be given you besides" (Mt 6:31–33).

Of course, in Jesus' own life his radical trust would lead him to the cross, believing that somehow the power of God's love is greater than death.

The Church and Moral Vision

Jesus' life and words provided his followers with a vision and principles for moral and spiritual life. He did not, however, address all the issues that would confront them throughout history. This is the task of the church guided by the Spirit. The church lives in the world, not apart from it, and its moral vision can be a light to the world. In order for this to be effective, Cardinal Joseph Bernardin of Chicago has suggested that the church must adopt a consistent ethic of life. The church must be recognized as a place where human life and dignity are actively supported in the world and in the hard political and economic choices that confront us as a people. Bernardin argues that the moral vision of the gospel must be a "seamless garment" connecting all issues in which the existence or the dignity of human life is at stake. In an address at Fordham University, he addressed the need for all those involved in "pro-life" commitments to recognize the scope of such endeavors:

> If one contends, as we do, that the right of every fetus to be born should be protected by civil law and

61

supported by civil consensus, then our moral, political and economic responsibilities do not stop at the moment of birth. Those who defend the right to life of the weakest among us must be equally visible in support of the quality of life of the powerless among us: the old and the young, the hungry and the homeless, the undocumented immigrant and the unemployed worker. Such a quality of life posture translates into specific political and economic positions. . . .[1]

Bernardin is thus taking the moral vision of the gospel and applying it to the real world in which human beings live. Such a vision involves commitment to a wide variety of personal and social concerns.

Summary

1. For Christians, morality and conscience are rooted in the person and teaching of Jesus Christ.
2. Jesus offered a vision of life that called for conversion, a change of heart and a new way of living.
3. As children of the same "Abba," the human community must learn to live as brothers and sisters.
4. Jesus called his disciples to live for God's kingdom and not their own.
5. He insisted that love of God and love of others be united.
6. Love of neighbor had no boundaries for Jesus and even included enemies.
7. At the heart of the gospel is a proclamation of forgiveness.
8. Jesus identified with the weak and the oppressed and encouraged his disciples to do the same.
9. He insisted that love was more than lip service. It demanded real action.
10. Jesus called for not only outward behavior, but interior change of heart, a true conviction.

11. Jesus' life and message demands moral courage in a spirit of non-violence. It includes a willingness to confront evil with love.
12. To live such a life demands radical trust in God and in a future for human love.
13. Jesus lived what he taught, and his life is the model for all Christians: one lived in fidelity to God and in love for his brothers and sisters.
14. Christians today are challenged to live a consistent ethic of life, applying the moral vision of the gospel to personal and social problems of our age.

Questions for Review

1. What was Jesus' name for God and what does it reveal about his vision of life?
2. What is "conversion" as it is understood in the gospels?
3. What are some of the characteristics of God's reign that we find in the parables of Jesus?
4. What was unusual about Jesus' choice of the greatest of the commandments?
5. What is the meaning of the parable of the good Samaritan?
6. How did Jesus alienate the religious leaders of his time?
7. According to Matthew 25, what is the final criterion for judgment?
8. What is meant by moral courage and how did Jesus display it?
9. Explain Cardinal Bernardin's notion of a consistent ethic of life.

For Personal Reflection and Discussion

1. Conversion, change of heart, is never a once and for all reality. It is ongoing for a lifetime. Do you think that you have undergone "conversions" in your life? What have they been? Can you identify any area of your life currently in need of conversion?

2. What aspect of Jesus' teaching has stood out for you? Which of his sayings or parables have you always remembered? Which of his teachings has most confused you?

3. If Jesus walked the earth today, what do you think he would be doing and what would he be saying?

4. What do you think are the key areas of social concern for Christians today?

Suggested Reading

Matthew, Mark, Luke and John

Häring Bernard. *Free and Faithful in Christ, Vol 1*. New York: Crossroad, 1982 (especially Chapter 1).

5

Conscience and the Authority of the Church

In our attempt to describe conscience, we followed the lead of Fr. Timothy O'Connell in distinguishing three dimensions to conscience. The first and third of those dimensions are strongly individual. Conscience/1 recognizes the fundamental orientation to know and do the good. Conscience/3 recognizes both the gift and the burden of the individual's responsibility and judgment. This individualistic emphasis on conscience is seen also in the statement from the Second Vatican Council describing it as the place where one is *alone* with God. Yet, for all the truths that are spoken here, conscience is radically communal. If, as Fr. O'Connell asserts, conscience/2 must "bow at the altar of truth," then it must seek to know and learn the truth which can only be done in the context of others. The truth is something that one comes to discover only in community, in the world of relationships, thoughts, feelings, politics, work and social interaction. We learn from our parents, relatives, friends, teachers and communities. Within our world, certain people and groups establish privileged places for learning moral truth: the truth about the meaning of our lives and destiny. It is within this context that we must look at the role of Christian faith and the church.

Faith and Conversion

For most Christians, their religion and "faith" begins as an accident of birth. They were baptized as infants, brought into the church, and hence, without their willing or choosing, they became "Christians." However, as we have already seen, faith requires conversion, a personal choice and direction in one's life. Somewhere along the line we must ratify the faith that has been given to us. This is not simply to give intellectual assent to doctrinal propositions (such as accepting the divine nature of Jesus), but rather it also means to give personal assent to living the life of faith as well (spiritually and morally). Faith affects more than the way we think; it affects who we are and how we live.

This faith does not simply fall from the sky into our lives. It is gained from being exposed to a community of faith. Through this community we learn about values and a way of life as well as about doctrines and creeds. It is through a community that we "catch" the faith. For most people the primary teachers of this faith are their parents. Our faith is communicated in all the day to day ways of relating and being with one another. Beyond the parents, there is the local community of faith: the congregation or the parish. Within that community there may be special influences, perhaps a certain priest or teacher. All of these mentors of faith point beyond themselves to a larger reality that connects all of them together. They all point to the mystery of God alive in Jesus Christ and living in and through the church and the world. As we grow in our faith, we are able to expand the sources of our growth. We recognize that there is much to be learned from the faith of those outside the church, from the wisdom and goodness of friends and teachers, from heroes both past and present, from classic books and sources, from our own experience and that of others. We recognize that the goal is not to "keep the faith" as if were simply a series of religious obligations. Rather, like Jesus himself, we are to grow "steadily in wisdom and age and grace before God and men" (Lk 2:52).

For Christians, conscience is the way that we live our faith on our daily decisions. Conscience, for Christians, cannot be separated from faith. A healthy conscience will normally function reflexively, immediately responding to situations with the values that one has made a part of oneself. In some situations, however, conscience demands large, difficult and painstaking decisions. It is within this context that we look at the role of the teaching authority of the church in the formation of conscience. If conscience is radically communal, what role does the Christian community and the authority in the church play in that conscience?

Sources of Authority for Christian Conscience

The nature and role of authority in the formation of conscience is a difficult and controversial topic. As we have seen, the Catholic Church emphasizes the interrelationship between scripture and tradition as the great sources of authority. The scriptures provide the foundational cornerstone of faith, but they do not exist as documents of the past. They are a living word, and their interpretation and message has always been one that reflects new light on each age. The scriptures provide the principles of faith but certainly do not address all the issues that affect people today. This is the task of "tradition." It interprets and guides. It places the events of the present under the light of faith. Tradition is not merely a repetition of the past; that is traditionalism. It is, rather, a living faith that is handed down from one generation to the next. This living faith must always open itself to the new challenges of a new age. In order to better understand the nature of authority in the church, we will begin with the perspective of the New Testament.

Jesus and Authority

In the gospels, the teaching of Jesus is clear: authority and service are inseparable.

A dispute arose among them (the apostles) about who should be regarded as the greatest. He said:

67

"Earthly kings lord it over their people. Those who exercise authority over them are called their benefactors. Yet it cannot be that way with you. Let the greater among you be as the junior, the leader as the servant" (Lk 22:24–26).

Jesus' greatest conflicts were with those who exercised religious authority during his lifetime. Many had become preoccupied with the respect gained by their place of office and lost sight of the true meaning of the faith that they taught. Jesus criticized them as "blind guides" and hypocrites who subvert the heart of the law. John's gospel tells us that on the night before he died, at the last supper, Jesus rose from the meal and washed his apostles' feet saying to them, "You address me as 'Teacher' and 'Lord,' and fittingly enough, for that is what I am. But if I washed your feet—I who am Teacher and Lord—then you must wash each other's feet" (Jn 13:13–14). Jesus' example and his life are clear: moral and religious authority must be rooted in service to others.

The Holy Spirit: The Source of Authority in the Church

Christians do not believe that Jesus spent thirty years on earth and then returned to heaven. Rather, they believe that Christ continues to be present to the church in and through his Spirit. In John, Jesus says, "This much I have told you while I was still with you; the Paraclete, the Holy Spirit whom the Father will send in my name, will instruct you in everything and will remind you of all that I told you" (Jn 14:25–26).

Paul makes it clear that the locus of the Spirit is the entire church as the body of Christ. He explains that the church is composed of many different gifts, all of which come from the Spirit. "To each person the manifestation of the Spirit is given for the common good" (1 Cor 12:7). Within the diversity of the gifts, each member of the church has a role to play. Paul

68

goes on to say that the apostles enjoy a special status as leaders within the church, but he makes it clear that the greatest of the gifts of the Spirit is not apostleship but love:

> Now I will show you the way which surpasses all the others. If I speak with human tongues and angelic as well, but do not have love, I am a noisy gong, a clanging cymbal. If I have the gift of prophecy and with full knowledge comprehend all mysteries, if I have faith great enough to move mountains, but have not love, I am nothing" (1 Cor 13:1–2).

The Role of the Bishop in the Early Church

As the church expanded in the first century and began to look to a future, it became more organized. Thus, in some of the later epistles (particularly 1 and 2 Timothy and Titus) we find less emphasis on the gifts of the Spirit and more emphasis on providing stable structure and leadership for the community. In addition, the role of the new leaders of the communities was now to include maintaining the true seed of faith handed down from the apostles and in jeopardy of being destroyed by many "false teachers." The later New Testament epistles consistently address this theme. Leadership in the church quickly became more institutionalized, with the bishops of the local communities gaining tremendous authority.

The Magisterium and Conscience

The Catholic Church maintains that the hierarchical structure of the church is not simply a human invention, but rather something willed by Christ. Vatican II makes this eminently clear throughout its document on the church:

> Just as the role that the Lord gave individually to Peter, the first among the apostles, is permanent

and was meant to be transmitted to his successors, so also the apostles' office of nurturing the church is permanent, and was meant to be exercised without interruption by the sacred order of bishops. . . . He who hears them, hears Christ and he who rejects them, rejects Christ and the one who sent Christ" (*Lumen Gentium*, n. 20).

Thus the church as a people and an institution is governed by the college of bishops in communion with the pope. Each bishop is the head of a local diocese. The teaching authority of the bishops exists as a group only when in union with the pope, the bishop of Rome. "Together with its head, the Roman pontiff, and never without this head, the episcopal order is the subject of supreme and full power over the universal church" (*Lumen Gentium*, n. 20). However, as the head of the episcopal order the pope enjoys a status not given to any other bishop. "For, in virtue of his office, that is, as vicar of Christ and pastor of the whole church, the Roman pontiff has full, supreme and universal power over the church. And he can always exercise this power freely" (*Lumen Gentium*, n. 22).

Infallibility

One of the best known, most controversial, and least understood doctrines of the church is the infallible teaching authority of the pope. It is not uncommon to find among both Catholics and non-Catholics the idea that Catholics believe that the pope is infallible, as if it were a personal attribute. The word "infallible" means incapable of error, and thus only God can be said to be infallible. As it is applied to the pope, infallibility concerns his capacity to speak as head of the church concerning the fundamental truth of Christian faith and morals. The church believes that it is not simply a matter of opinion or a good idea to believe that Jesus is the Lord, the Savior, the Son of God. It believes that these assertions are true and revealed by God. Revelation is not arbitrary, and it belongs to the teaching office of the pope to be able to declare what is not arbitrary and what is revealed. Thus, the infallibility enjoyed by the pope is really derived from the promise of the Holy Spirit to the entire church. He speaks as the head of the church, *ex cathedra* as it is called. Vatican II stated the doctrine of infallibility in the *Dogmatic Constitution on the Church*:

> This infallibility with which the divine Redeemer willed his church to be endowed in defining a doctrine of faith and morals extends as far as the deposit of divine revelation, which must be religiously guarded and faithfully expounded. This is the infallibility which the Roman pontiff, the head of the college of bishops, enjoys in virtue of his office, when as the supreme shepherd and teacher of all the faithful, who confirms his brethren in their faith, he proclaims by a definitive act some doctrine of faith and morals. . . . For then the Roman pontiff is not pronouncing judgment as a private person. Rather, as the supreme teacher of the universal church, as one in whom the charism of the infallibility of the church is individually present, he is expounding or developing a doctrine of Catholic faith (*Lumen Gentium*, n. 25).

Note the following elements of this passage:
1. Infallibility, as a charism or gift of the Spirit, belongs to the church as a whole as well as to the teaching office of the pope.
2. Infallible teachings are limited to the "deposit of divine revelation"—those beliefs and teachings that are essential to the faith, an area that is not clearly distinguished anywhere. They are never the private opinions of the man.
   Infallibility in the church is not limited to the pope alone. It belongs as well to the entire body of bishops when they

71

teach in union with the pope concerning matters of faith and morals. This authority can be exercised by their concurrence on essential matters or when they are formally gathered in an ecumenical council (*Lumen Gentium*, n. 25).

Likewise, the entire faithful are considered infallible when, "from the bishops down to the last member of the laity, it shows universal agreement in matters of faith and morals" (*Lumen Gentium*, n. 12).

Fallibility

If we examine closely the nature of infallibility in the church, in the bishops and in the pope, we can see that it will be the exception and not the rule in matters of church teaching. Most of what is infallible has never been so declared by the pope. Certainly the belief that Jesus is the Lord and savior is an infallible teaching of the church as a whole, but statements of infallibility are almost non-existent. (In 1950, Pius XII declared the assumption of Mary to be an infallible teaching of the church. There are probably no other examples of papal infallibility.)

In areas of morality, infallibility becomes even more problematic. The pope has never spoken infallibly on any moral issue. Some theologians believe that the only moral areas that could possibly be declared infallible are broad statements of principles and not specific actions. Essentially the magisterium of the church when teaching on matters of morals is in fact fallible. This does not mean that it is wrong. It means that it is *capable* of being wrong. Nor does it mean that its teaching is simply another voice among many. To the contrary, the teaching of the pope and bishops on moral issues must always be given great priority in the formation of a Christian's conscience. "In matters of faith and morals the bishops speak in the name of Christ and the faithful are to accept their teaching and adhere to it with a religious assent of soul. This religious submission of will and of mind must be shown in a special way to the Roman pontiff, even when he is not speaking ex cathedra" (*Lumen Gentium*, n. 25).

Assent and Dissent

Taken at face value, this statement from Vatican II seems to place obedience and loyalty as the highest Christian virtues. Here we must ask the question, "What is meant by religious assent of soul and religious submission of will and mind?" This is a question of interpretation. Some theologians emphasize the responsibility to defer to the teaching of the church; others emphasize the importance of genuine assent.

The statements clearly ask for more than simple or blind obedience. Civil laws ask for obedience. It is unimportant whether or not one assents to the law; one must obey it. But this is not the case in the teaching of the church. Rather, "religious assent of soul" indicates a union with the church, an interior assent, a joining of one's mind and heart with the mind and heart of the church. This should be the way that faith normally works. The teaching of the magisterium will normally "ring true" to the person because they are joined on the level of faith. Such assent is "religious" because it respects the inherent authority of the pope and bishops to teach on behalf of the church. In his book entitled *Magisterium: Teaching Authority in the Catholic Church*, Francis A. Sullivan, S.J. states the issue this way:

> . . . the response called for by the authoritative magisterium is not the relatively simple obedience of the will, but the complicated business of "obedience of judgment."[1]

A "religious submission of mind and will" refers to a willingness to view one's own thoughts and opinions in light of the teaching authority of the church. It begins with respect for the magisterium's role as teacher and an openness to understand and accept its position. It respects the authority of the pope and bishops to speak on behalf of the believing community. This "religious submission" refers to an attitude of humility, genuinely seeking the truth, being open to being taught by others and realizing the fallibility of one's own positions.

What, then, if one possesses such an attitude but genuinely cannot assent? In fact, the person is convinced that the magisterium is wrong. Is it possible to dissent from the teachings of the church and still remain a good Catholic? As we have seen, ultimately one must obey his or her conscience. The same council that speaks of "assent" and "submission" also speaks of the sanctity of conscience. Yet it is only the genuine Christian conscience (one that sincerely seeks the truth in light of the gospel, consults the teaching of the church, thinks, prays) that may dissent. As we have seen, one may not appeal to conscience as a form of isolation. One of the best signs for a dissenting conscience is the existence of dissent in the lives of other Christians who are genuinely seeking to live the faith deeply. Dissent from church teaching should be seen as an exception that one undertakes with hesitation. In dissenting, one must also recognize the fallibility of one's own conscience and be willing to reevaluate the decision. Ultimately, Christians are called to follow their master in seeking above all else the will of God.

The question of dissent is a hotly debated one within the church. "Conservative" theologians tend to emphasize the responsibility of the faithful to give assent to the teaching of the church, and seem to fear the mentality that will always see itself as the exception to the rule. The documents of Vatican II do not directly address the issue of dissent from within the church. When such questions were raised, the commission said that one should consult "the approved authors," meaning the moral texts used in seminary training. When such authors are consulted, one may always find a carefully nuanced description of the right to dissent from non-infallible teachings.[2]

Method and Morality

At the heart of the debate on the nature of authority in the church is the question of method for making moral decisions (or for doing moral theology). For hundreds of years the church depended on a "classicist" method. From this perspective, truth is an absolute and universal phenomenon known to the mind of God. This truth is conveyed by God to the church through the pope and bishops, and the faithful learn the truth by listening to the magisterium. Within this perspective, something is right or wrong, not because of its inherent truth or value, but because the church says that it is right or wrong. Its truth is derived from its authority. The bishops and pope spoke on behalf of Christ and Christ spoke on behalf of God the Father. This method is generally unacceptable to people today. An "historical consciousness" dominates human thinking today. We are aware of how values and laws are shaped by people, circumstances, cultures, time and place. Right and wrong are not determined simply by the weight of authority but by the human spirit capable of discerning human value. Thus the community as a whole becomes the focus for determining values. This does not detract from the authority of the pope and bishops. They do indeed teach on behalf of the church. However, for such teaching to be effective today, it is necessary that it appeal to the minds, heart and soul of the faithful and not simply to their own authority. The truth of what they speak, while not totally limited to their understanding of the issue, must be communicated in such a way that others may truly learn from and be enlightened by it.

Church and Conscience: Different Perspectives

In order to understand the relationship between church and conscience, much will depend on one's understanding of the church and the nature and role of authority within the church. Fr. Avery Dulles has written an extraordinarily influential book entitled *Models of the Church*, in which he examines five different perspectives or "models" for understanding the church. In briefly looking at each, we will try to discern how they could affect one's understanding of conscience. He describes the church as an institution, as a community, as a sacrament, as a herald and as a servant.

The church, as an institution, is an organization consisting of an authority structure (a hierarchy), doctrines, laws and dogmas. The key to an institution is the structure that it provides. Institutions very often shape the people that serve. The Catholic Church has a particularly strong institutional dimension. The pope and bishops together form the magisterium, the official teaching office of the church. It is their task to teach in the name of the entire church. Thus, the Second Vatican Council declared that the "bishops, the successors of the apostles, who, together with the successor of Peter, the vicar of Christ and the visible head of the whole church, govern the house of the living God" (*Lumen Gentium*, n. 18).

Within this perspective, conscience will give particular weight to the teaching of the pope and the bishops on moral issues. One of the major values of conscience in this model will be *loyalty*. A danger of this view is to confuse conscience with simple, unthinking obedience.

Dulles' second model is community. Here the focus is on the church as a people. The church is not primarily laws, obligations, rituals, priests and bishops. It is the entire people of God united in their faith in Christ and in love and service to one another. The church shifts from "they" to "we." Using St. Paul's image of the church as the body of Christ, the Second Vatican Council declared:

> As all the members of the human body, though they are many, form one body, so also are the faithful in Christ. Also in the building up of Christ's body there is a flourishing variety of members and functions. There is only one Spirit who, according to his own richness and the needs of the ministries, distributes

his gifts for the welfare of the church (*Lumen Gentium*, n. 7).

One of the major strengths of such a perspective is its diversity and richness. Here conscience will be particularly sensitive to the *wisdom within the entire community* and be more at home with pluralism within the church community itself. One of the dangers of this model is to lose a sense of unifying identity in which all voices within the church take on equal weight and importance.

The third model is that of sacrament, and it is the most abstract and difficult to explain. Within this model the church is seen as a "sign" of Christ's presence in the world. Through its entire life the church makes Christ present in the world. As such, it is a sacrament of Christ in the world. Within this model the seven sacraments take on special importance as unique moments of grace. "Truly partaking of the body of the Lord in the breaking of the eucharistic bread, we are taken up into communion with him and with one another" (*Lumen Gentium*, n. 7). Conscience here will be understood in the context of a *sacramental spirituality* and will emphasize the importance of the eucharist and penance (and, in many cases, marriage) as guides to discerning the Spirit. The danger of such a model is a tendency to become parochial and isolated from other sources of wisdom.

The fourth model is called a "herald." The main role of the church is to proclaim its faith in Jesus Christ. It is an evangelical model in which the Bible takes on special importance. Conscience is understood within the context of one's personal relationship with Jesus Christ. The emphasis is on the individual as he or she is challenged to conversion by the word of God. Authority is rooted in the *word of God*. In its document on revelation, the Second Vatican Council declared that the Scriptures must be taken together with sacred tradition as the supreme rule of faith. "For, inspired by God and committed once and for all to writing, they impart the word of God himself without change, and make the voice of the Holy Spirit resound in the words of the prophets and the apostles" (n. 21). One of the weaknesses of the herald model is a tendency to isolate the scriptures from the rest of the believing community and to ignore the Spirit speaking today in the world.

The fifth and final model is the servant model. From this perspective, the role of the church is to serve the world. It is to place itself in service to those most in need. The focus of the church is not to be on itself but on others, particularly the poor and the oppressed. Conscience then is always asking itself what it has done for the least of God's children. It is often a prophetic, counter-cultural stance taken on behalf of those living on the margins of society. It measures itself by a love that shows itself in *justice* and often makes use of contemporary forms of social analysis. This model was given great encouragement in the *Pastoral Constitution on the Church in the Modern World* and official status within the church at the International Synod of Bishops in 1974 which declared that the task of working for justice constitutes an essential element of preaching the gospel. A possible weakness of such an approach is to lose a sense of what makes this specifically *Christian* conscience and to identify the role of the church with political goals and achievements.

Model	*Dominant Values*	*Possible Dangers*
1. Institution	identity, loyalty, clarity	authoritarian, moralistic
2. Community	pluralism, diversity, human experience	rivalries, lack of identity
3. Sacrament	rich spirituality and tradition, deeply symbolic	isolated from the world, own unique language

Model	Dominant Values	Possible Dangers
4. Herald	word of God, biblical values	isolated from world, tendency to fundamentalism
5. Servant	justice, peace, love in action	identify with political ideology, lose spiritual roots

Which is the "correct" model for interpreting the church? None and all. One of the points that Dulles wishes to make is that the church is too rich a mystery to be simply explained by any one of these dimensions. To some extent they all function together. If we examine the strengths of each model, we may come up with the following characteristics concerning conscience and the church. First, conscience exists within a community of believers. Individual conscience is not the same as isolated conscience which is thoroughly non-Christian. Second, the entire community of believers is the main source of moral wisdom. Conscience is formed not solely by the magisterium but by the real values and wisdom of the entire community. Third, the pope and bishops play a special role within this community as those entrusted with the office of teaching on behalf of the entire church. Fourth, the entire community, including the magisterium, must place themselves and their decisions before the word of God. The scriptures have a unique normative role in determining Christian morality. Fifth, Christian conscience must always be understood within the context of Christian faith and spirituality. Sixth, Christian conscience must always be oriented by the great virtues of love and justice. Seventh, conscience is not an escape from the world but service to the world. Eighth, conscience must be open to the many sources of moral wisdom and truth that lie outside the church. It must be ecumenical in spirit.

Summary

1. Conscience is radically communal. It is formed and informed by all the sources of truth within the human community.
2. Christian conscience is linked to Christian faith and formed by it.
3. The entire Christian community plays a critical role within the formation of conscience, with parents enjoying a preeminent role in the formation of a child's conscience
4. The magisterium—the pope and the bishops—exercises a special ministry to teach on behalf of the church.
5. The Catholic Church believes in the infallible teaching authority of the pope as derived from the infallibility of the church and Christ's gift of the Spirit.
6. Papal infallibility has never been formally declared concerning a moral issue.
7. Catholic Christians are called to give 'assent" and not mere obedience to the teaching of the magisterium.
8. Dissent should be a rare exception with a church that is functioning healthily.
9. Freedom to dissent in the church is limited to those cases where the person genuinely believes that the call of love, justice and the truth demand it.
10. Different views of the church lead to different perspectives on conscience. An institutional emphasis focuses on loyalty. A community model is more at home with plurality. The sacramental model focuses on spirituality. Herald emphasizes the authority of the Bible. The servant model focuses on the need to create a better world. Each has a truth to offer and dangers to avoid.

Questions for Review

1. In what sense is conscience very private and personal? How is it communal?
2. What was Jesus' view of the nature of authority?

3. Explain Paul's image of the church as the body of Christ? According to Paul, which is the greatest of the gifts of the Holy Spirit?
4. What is the magisterium in the church? Who comprise the magisterium?
5. What is meant by papal infallibility? Under what conditions is the pope considered to be able to teach infallibly? What moral issues have been declared infallible?
6. What role does the teaching of the magisterium play in the conscience of a Catholic Christian?
7. Under what circumstances might a Catholic dissent from the teaching of the church?
8. Briefly explain each of Dulles' five models of the church and how they would influence a person's understanding of conscience?

For Personal Reflection and Discussion

Read the church's teaching on one of the following issues, and research the reaction to the position from theologians within the church.

1. "Humanae Vitae" (1968), Pope Paul VI's encyclical on marital love, reproduction and birth control.
2. "Declaration on Certain Questions Concerning Sexual Ethics" (1975).
3. Instruction of the Congregation for the Doctrine of Faith regarding reproductive technologies (March 1987).

Suggested Reading

Dulles, Avery. *Models of the Church*. Image Books, Doubleday, 1978.

Sullivan, Francis. *Magisterium: Teaching Authority in the Catholic Church*. Paulist Press, 1983.

Curran, C. and R. McCormick, eds. *Readings in Moral Theology No. 3: The Magisterium and Morality*. Paulist Press, 1982.

Notes

Chapter 1

1. Timothy O'Connell, *Principles for a Catholic Morality* (New York: The Seabury Press, 1976), pp. 83–97.
2. *Ibid.* pp. 144–154.
3. See Richard Viladesau, *The Reason for Our Hope* (New York/Ramsey: Paulist Press, 1984), pp. 177–183.
4. Abraham H. Maslow, *Toward a Psychology of Being* (New York: Van Nostrand Reinhold, 1968), p. 60.

Chapter 2

1. John Glaser, "Conscience and Superego: A Key Distinction," in *Conscience: Theological and Psychological Perspectives*, C. Ellis Nelson ed. (New York/Paramus/Toronto: Newman Press, 1973), pp. 175–176.
2. Bernard Häring, *Free and Faithful in Christ, Vol. 1* (New York: Crossroad, 1982), p. 235.

Chapter 3

1. Pope John Paul II, *Solicitudo Rei Socialis*, reprinted in *Origins*, March 3, 1988, Vol. 17. No. 38.
2. Eugene Kennedy, *A Sense of Life, A Sense of Sin* (Garden City: Image Books, 1975), p. 55.

Chapter 4

1. From an address delivered at Fordham University and reprinted in *Origins*, December 29, 1983, Vol. 13. No. 29.

Chapter 5

1. Francis A. Sullivan, *Magisterium* (New York/Ramsey: Paulist Press, 1983), p. 162.

2. Cf. Joseph A. Komonchak, "Ordinary Papal Magisterium and Religious Assent," in *Readings in Moral Theology No. 3*, C. Curran and R. McCormick, eds. (New York/Ramsey: Paulist Press, 1982), pp. 67–90.